Morning Messages
"We Are Here" Transmissions

Morning Messages "We Are Here" Transmissions
Written by Peggy Black in partnership with the 'team'

Book and Cover Design, Graphics:
Peggy Black and Melanie Gendron

Melanie Gendron
Gendron Studios
P. O. Box 1438
Felton, CA. 95018
www.melaniegendron.com
gentarot@comcast.net
831-335-9064

Publisher: Motivational Press, Inc
7668 El Camino Real #104-223
Carlsbad, CA 92009
www.MotivationalPress.com

Peggy Black: Transducer, Scribe and Witness
Executive Producer, Cover Design, Transmissions, Drawings
Morning Messages, P. O. Box 199, Felton, CA. 95018
www.morningmessages.com
joyandgratitude@aol.com
831-335-3145

ISBN: 978-1-935723-080

Manufactured in the United States of America

Testimonies from Readers...

I thought I was pretty "in tune" with the Universe. YOU, on the other hand, have opened a whole new area of my consciousness and I love it. —Sincerely, Janet

Thank you for your wonderful messages. I found a piece of the puzzle after many years of searching. Your messages resonated with me so profoundly that I was overwhelmed with tears of emotions. —Blessings, Donna—Spain

Through the 12 years I have been on a spiritual path, one of my strong desires has been for my skeptical, analytically-minded husband to become more spiritually like-minded. Many times when I would share non-traditional spiritual thoughts with him, he would roll his eyes and walk out of the room shaking his head. Eventually, we progressed to the point where he would roll his eyes but stay in the room and talk about it. And now FINALLY, he has found something that he resonates with: Your Morning Messages!! YAY!! I am so thrilled, and that is putting it mildly. —Jenny

Beautiful Soul, thank you, thank you, thank you for these valuable words heart to heart thank you. —Shebl—Egypt

I really appreciate, anticipate and cherish these messages. These are some of the most profound and stirring messages I have ever read, these are priceless. Thanks for all you do. —Roger

Thank you for the faithful morning messages which opens fountains of treasures inside of me. —Great light to you, Karin—Sweden

For those of us who are dragging our feet through the mire striving to reach higher consciousness, the morning message is an inspiration to strive for another day. —Mark

As an Agape member and student of metaphysics for over 30 years, I have seen and read a lot of "channeled" work. BUT YOURS, what comes through you has an extraordinary frequency to it. It feels like the Brotherhood of Light. You are saturating the quantum field more than you know. —Bless you, Laressa

You give me a lot of strength and remind me who I am. —Miriam—Jerusalem

Thank you for the wonderful messages. I had a crummy day, broke something, fought with my husband, kicked the shampoo and hurt my toe, meltdown... slogging through emails and coming upon a Morning Message: Voila! Instant shift in energy. More email: the world's a mess, everyone wants time, money: another Morning Message and I feel my breathing change and my shoulder muscles relax. More e-mails—frustration, impatience, complaining. And another Morning Message: another shift in energy, and relief to remember the power of love and gratitude, and an open heart.— Thank you, lw

The deepness of the morning messages really remind me of the Wingmakers material, less aimed at the mind but straight to the heart. —Thank you, Guido—Holland

Dear Peggy, your messages moved me so much and rings true... like Eileen Caddy's from the Findhorn foundation in Scotland.— Martine—Switzerland

The Morning Messages never fail to uplift me, teach me and encourage me to continue working with and listening to my own inner guidance. —Love, Lisa

I love the messages. They are of great value and help to me to stay in balance and filled with love in this challenging time. —Estera— Slovenia

The "truth" of this morning message went through me like a lightening bolt; it was the reading of the message that flipped the switch on! —Very, Very Cool, Christopher

Peggy, in the past 15 plus years I have had more healing, activations, transmissions, attunements, mastery sessions, clearing regressions, etc. than you can imagine. This session with you and the Team has definitely been among the most powerful. —Thank you, Cathy

I am grateful and now have unbelievable tools. You are in complete integrity and clean as a whistle as a channel. The team is so respectful and in utter integrity. I love that they say "we invite you". What a respectful and agenda-less way of encouraging change. —Rhonda

Praise for the Morning Messages...

Peggy's team invites each of us to expand and embrace a more divine aspect of ourselves. These messages speak a spiritual, energetic language, awakening inner awareness and growth. Don't miss them.

> —Virginia Essene, author of *New Teaching for an Awakening Humanity* and eight other titles

Morning Messages "We Are Here" Transmissions' time has come. You'll feel the wisdom, love and energy in every inspiring word. Allow them to light your path. Thank you, Peggy Black, for your commitment to our universal family!

> —Donna Aazura, Best selling co-author of *How Did You Do That!*

This is one of those rare occasions were a high caliber, mystical transmission is delivered in simple and practical language for easy assimilation.

> —Cyndi Silva, MetaphysicalWisdom.com

I have known Peggy Black for a number of years and watched her LIGHT grow in the world, like the dawn grows into high noon. She is a clear, loving devoted servant to LOVE and LIGHT on all levels. Her Morning Messages are touching the lives of many. Bless you Peggy for the gift you are in life.

> —Kay Snow-Davis, international author and facilitator of 'Soul Purpose Living.'

Peggy Black brings forth gems of personal insight that can transform your perspective about yourself, your relationships and your world. We have found that changing your viewpoint in small ways each day can have a powerful impact upon how your life unfolds. Reading and contemplating her Morning Messages will lead to an inner awakening that enriches your life in unexpected ways.

> —Jerry and Richela Chapman, authors of *Through the Veil* and *One Speaks.*

Morning Messages inspire people to shift their reality in a positive direction. The playful yet practical messages help us positively transform our perspective, and thereby our approach to life.

> —Cynthia Sue Larson, author of *Aura Advantage*

Peggy Black's morning messages are the only way to start the day. Find peace when you see them. These are your secrets to success!

—Jill Lublin, international speaker and best selling author, *Guerrilla Publicity, Networking Magic* and *Get Noticed... Get Referrals*

Images of beings from an inner world combine with sunrise messages so rich and timeless... The result brings a smile to my soul... Open this book to any page and smile for yourself.

—Peter Melton, author of *Waves of Oneness*

Since the very first moment Morning Messages made their way into my awareness, I have incorporated their powerful messages into my daily spiritual practice. Beyond inspirational, they are transformational in their simplicity and ability to zone in on the truth and task at hand. Thank you, dear Peggy, for your wonderful frequency of love that makes you so accessible for your powerful team to support us on our earthly journeys. They have changed our lives forever! In Complete Gratitude,

—Marcy Neumann, President, Heartlites Incorporated

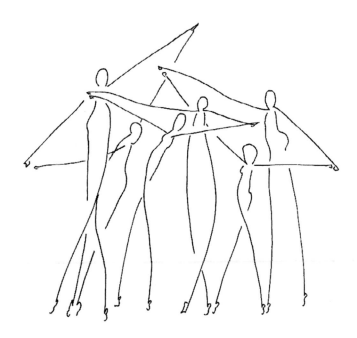

Gratitudes and Appreciation...

This opportunity of bringing Morning Messages, "We Are Here" Transmissions to the global community has opened and expanded my life and my heart.

I have been privileged to witness and experience the blessings, synchronicities and miracles that have embraced every aspect of the process. There has been a graceful flow of support always coming in such timely and appropriate ways.

I value a very special team of friends who have gifted me their support, time and encouragement. Their generosity of spirit and funding made this global offering possible. They have been on board since the first Message, assisting me with the process, anchoring the experience with intentions and clarity. They are my cosmic sisters and forever friends providing a loving, conscious foundation. I gratefully thank Barbara, Ellen, Jennifer, Judy, Susana, Jane, Amrita and Janice W.

I honor with joy and gratitude my precious and wise daughters Devi, Cheri and Becki for their loving acceptance and sage advice.

I acknowledge another empowering team for their support: Randy, Joanna, Janice A, Leigh, Melanie, Nicole, Datta, Brian, Peter, Tom, Michael, Neil, Lida, Michelle, and all the beautiful women in my Miracle Intention support group. I thank all those named and unnamed who have offered assistance, the perfect gift at the perfect time.

I want to lovingly thank the family of subscribers. Your personal stories of how the Messages touched your life have been an inspiration for me to continue. It has been an honor to serve all the individuals in personal readings. A special thanks to all who made donations and to the precious sponsors for their financial gifts and trust, may you be blessed abundantly.

I am grateful for my deep connection to Divine Source in all its manifestations. I am grateful for "my team" who continue to offer their love, wisdom and guidance, reminding me to stay in my heart.

"All success in life comes from the generous support and love of our friends." —blessings of grace and joy, Peggy

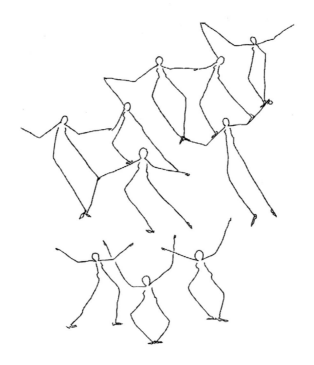

Dedication

It is an honor to dedicate this work to my incredible daughters
Devi, Cheri and Becki, who continue to inspire me,
and to my grandchildren Nathan, Brian, Emily and Bella
who enrich my life.

It is also offered in tenderhearted memory and deepest gratitude
to my beloved mother for her unconditional love,
to Merlino who opened all the doors,
and to my wise friend and mentor Rod, who saw me.

Morning Messages
"We Are Here" Transmissions
Wisdom and Guidance for Multidimensional Humans

by Peggy Black
in partnership with the 'team'

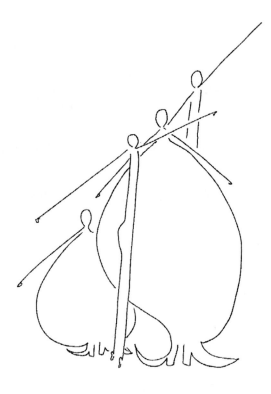

Contents...

Morning Messages Transmissions...

Foreward...

Beloveds, we are awakening to a One Heart World. This is the yearning of our Divine nature. Peggy Black and the "We Are Here" Team eloquently invites us ever more deeply into this experience. By allowing these transmissions to open our hearts, we find ourselves immersed in a resonant field overflowing with wise guidance, and a gentle beckoning to shift beyond what has been...to embrace and BE the Great-Full-Ness of Life.

Collectively, we are shifting from a paradigm of competition to one of Cooperation. In this Great Shift, we find ourselves treading unknown territory. Living in the mystery, one might say. Yet, as the veils of separation dissolve to reveal Unity, Connection and Oneness, we remember to celebrate our commonalities and support one another's brilliance and unique gifts. This is the Great Coming Together spoken of in multitudes of wisdom traditions throughout all time.

The "We Are Here" team invites us to open our hearts and swim together in the conscious fields of creation. To turn our gaze to the stars and remember we, too, are flow-ers of Life, shining the Light of Love for all to see.

As we immerse ourselves in these vibrations of wise words born of Love, Joy and Gratitude, we bridge the gap between Heaven and Earth, making the two One, witnessing ourselves stepping into an ever unfolding dance.

Peggy's ability to serve as a Scribe and Witness, to receive and record transmissions of wisdom, compassion, truth, joy and gratitude creates a sacred space of reflection: an opportunity to dance with the ineffable and experience for ourselves the Cosmic Beauty of an Awakened Heart. Celebrate this day, this moment, and remember all things are sacred, especially the gift of Life!

May these messages nourish your Soul. May they open doors and pathways previously unknown, clearing the way to reveal the intimate relationship between ourselves and the natural world — our Spirits and that of Mother Earth, our connection to Source and to One another.

Allow the sacred space created by the "We Are Here" team to ignite a deep remembrance of who you truly are — A Divine manifestation of Unconditional Love. You are here to shine, to thrive, and to gratefully offer your peace and joy to support the Great Shift of the Ages, and facilitate the continuance of Life.

For our children, for our ancestors, for all those to come and All that will BE — may we find the courage to shine our brilliant Light and enter the Age of Peace and Illumination as One. Together, as One Heart, One Mind, One Spirit.

Enjoy the journey... May Peace flow!

Stacey Robyn
Steward, *Go Gratitude!*

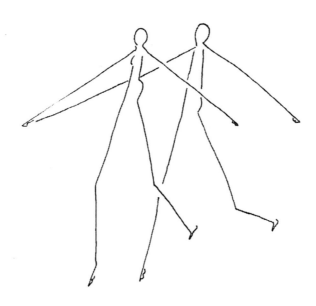

The Unfolding Process...

I was an only child who, like many children, was extremely open and receptive. I was clairvoyant, clairaudient, clairsentient. It was a difficult childhood because I could sense and see things that others couldn't, and I felt the feelings of others, owning them as my feelings. I had no idea that this was unusual since I had no reference point. Everyone just labeled me emotional, and moody, since I would cry at the drop of hat.

I remember asking my mother one day when I was about five, "What do I do when I hear someone call my name in my head?" She wisely said, "Answer them." She had premonitions and visions, as did my grandmother, and my aunt was known in the family as a healer.

It has taken me most of my adult life to begin to understand some of the natural abilities that were operating within. I tried many things and many times to shut these sensitivities down. It was very emotional and often painful. I rode this emotional roller coaster, not realizing that most of the emotions I was feeling and acting out were not even mine. I was sensing the emotions that other people would suppress and not allow themselves to feel.

I began to search for answers, and as I read books about others who were also sensitive, I began to grow in my understanding of self. I began to accept and acknowledge these sensitivities as the true gifts that they were. I began to recognize them and understand how to manage them. However, it has taken many years of struggle to appreciate, honor and be at peace with these abilities, and to maintain a balance and comfort with myself.

In the mid-seventies, when I was teaching a class in visual poise, I realized that most women, including myself, did not use one side of the body naturally and well. So I suggested to my class that we all practice using our less dominant hand to do mundane tasks. I decided for myself to use my left hand to draw. I gathered the usual tools: a sketch book and easy flowing pen. I spent hours allowing my left hand to just draw. I had no judgment or criticism, just acceptance and amazement, as images began to appear on the page. This was the birth of my line drawings, my stick figures.

They danced on the page. They flew, they gathered, they grouped. They became my friends and my passion. I allowed my left hand to totally express these delightful images, filling volumes of art books.

Then, my life dramatically changed with the end of my twenty year relationship with my first love, my husband and the father of my three daughters. After our divorce, we continued to share holidays and family events in support of the girls. Everything about my life had shifted in a totally different direction than I could have ever imagined.

I moved to the redwoods, bought a cottage and began to heal. Surrounded by nature, working in the garden, my sensitivities were gently awakened from years of misunderstanding and suppression. I again began to see and sense things that were invisible to others. I began to understand and became more comfortable with my inner knowing and inner guidance. Yet even in my healing process, I was unaware that I was carefully repressing my deepest grief and sense of loss.

When that little cottage burned to the ground, I found this incredible strength and determination, and I rebuilt my home. This process took several years and offered its own lessons of tenacity and focus. I gardened, I watched the sunrises, connecting with the energy and realms of nature. I began to open to my gifts and serve others. Guidance has been offered to me throughout my life — those moments when I would sense a presence, hear a voice, see an image or feel tingling in my body. I was now moving into a place of honoring and learning more about who I was as a woman, a human, and a divine spirit.

I worked in a health spa and offered reflexology and massage, during which I was able to see or sense what was happening in my clients' bodies. I had visions, like watching a movie of their life, when I would begin to work with them. This process was always amazing, actually a bit startling, yet I continued to allow it to unfold.

After thirteen years of being single, I remarried and began another thirteen year chapter of my life. It was a passionate and tumultuous relationship. I felt myself once again disappearing into someone else's reality, honoring their likes and dislikes and losing some aspect of my self. I was also aware that I was closing down parts of that independent woman I had discovered in my years alone. In order to stay in the relationship, I once again was blocking my sensitivity. Yet I continued to strive to make this relationship work.

In 1994, I returned from a year in Saudi Arabia and ended my second marriage. The devastation of another divorce was so crushing for me and the emotions so strong, that I was inspired to make my deep feelings of grief and sadness holy. So when an intense emotion would move through me, I would go to the closet where I had my altar. Lighting a candle and requesting that the divine transform this grief and sadness that I was offering as a gift to be uplifted, I would cry, wail and sob, until empty of that wave of emotion.

This was a powerful alchemical process, connecting with divine source and, as a sacred act, releasing the emotions of rage, guilt and sorrow as they moved through my body and mind. Offering these painful emotions as a gift to be transformed, I would scream my rage and moan my sorrow. Over time I realized I was literally clearing the emotions held in my body and memory that had never been expressed, from my first divorce, my childhood trauma, from my pain. Each and every time I offered my emotions, felt and expressed them fully as a sacred action and sacred offering, there was a tremendous release and expansion, like the opening of a door within.

Several months later I was astonished one day when, working with a client, these powerful and incredible sounds spontaneously began to be voiced through me. My energy and bodywork shifted to offering sounds as a healing modality. My clients were experiencing wonderful results from these sound vibrations and I was experiencing this awesome energy presence and connection.

Once I overcame my shyness and resistance to making these odd and unusual sounds in public, it became my passion as I was guided to remember the power of sound, frequency and vibrations. I was given the opportunities, the invitations, and total funding to travel to sacred sites and offer these sounds. You might say I traveled all over the world on sound vibrations. I joined the worldwide community of individuals who were offering sound vibrations as an accepted healing practice. This work and passion continued for eleven years. I became comfortable with the guidance and support I was receiving. I was offering my service and time to this mission and gift.

Little did I know that things were about to make a significant shift. I had been sensing for several months that my guidance wanted to work with me in a new way. So before I opened that door, I decided to bring some clarity to our arrangement. I actually wrote a mission statement.

Mission Statement of Celestial Contact and Partnership— In Co-Partnership/Fellowship, Connection We Work Together; We Serve Divine Love and Divine Light in the Awakening, Uplifting and Empowerment of Others.

We Create and Allow the Delicious Synchronicity to Weave the Manifestation of Our Goals and Intentions with Harmony, Balance, Ease, Grace, Joy and Delight.

We Work Together to Create the Balance, Smooth, Integraded Unfolding, the Clear and Authentic Synergy of This My Divine Work and Divine Purpose.

It is My Intention to Serve as a Speaker, a Receiver of Transmissions of Information, Images, and Visions. It is My Intention to Be a Spokesperson, Writer and Teacher in This Physical Reality and Time Frame for This Partnership/ Fellowship. It is My Intention to Be Fair Witness. It is My Intention to Be a Clear and Pure Channel of Divine Light and Divine Love.

In This Partnership, I Will Have Full Support in All Areas that I Need. It Will Be Arranged and Synchronized for My Financial Income to Continue to Increase Abundantly. I will Experience Total Financial Abundance and Security.

I Am Grateful That I Am Always Under the Law of Divine Protection and Divine Guidance in All Dimensions, Time-Frames and Realities. So Be It and So It is.

I did not realize while drafting my statement how incredibly my life was about to change. On February 5, 2005, I sat at my dining table where I could watch the sunrise; I read the mission statement; and then with more than a bit of attitude, I wrote "Contact" in my journal. The immediate response within my mind was *"We Are Here"*, and then the dialog began. I would ask a question and the answer would come. It was a very strange sensation, and I was extremely skeptical about what was happening. Yet for the next few weeks, I would be at the table where I could watch the sunrise and allow this contact to unfold. Later in the day, I would type the messages into my computer.

After several weeks of doing this, one foggy morning I just went upstairs and sat down at the computer. I started out with the statement that I was not sure this method would work. The response from the 'team' was *"The method is more an issue for you."* I responded that the view wasn't as nice from my desk as it was downstairs. They then invited me to make the view from my desk as pleasant as possible. So within a few days, I had a large branch removed from the oak tree just outside my office which had been blocking the sunrise and the stunning vista. I hung birdfeeders, added a birdbath and potted plants to the upper deck, creating a beautiful lush green garden and bird sanctuary.

Each morning I was dedicated to be at my desk to witness the sunrise. This time of the morning was quiet and I was more receptive. I started out describing the weather and the view in general, then would state my own emotional weather condition, the personal issues I might be experiencing. Next I would type Contact and the 'team' would respond with *"We are here"* and it would begin. They would focus the flow of information addressing my emotional weather condition and the issues I was dealing with. Their comments and sharing would be personal for me and yet their message always expanded to include the collective. Usually I stayed connected for over an hour each morning, resulting in several pages of transmissions or downloads.

This became my pattern for months and I was very selective with whom I shared what was happening. I was still a bit amazed, skeptical and cautious. After ten months or so, I was ordering the book *Go Gratitude* over the phone. I asked the gentleman I was speaking with how he had become involved with the Go Gratitude project. He shared that his company had published the book as well as created a presence on the internet with this global idea. I heard my 'team' state *"Tell him about the messages."* This request was so strong that without question, I told this stranger that I had been receiving these messages. He invited me to send him some examples. So with the 'team's' guidance, I selected several of the morning transmissions and sent them. It was days later he responded with his phone number and a request to please call immediately.

His name was Peter, and he informed me that his company wanted to work with me. They would create a website, a Flash movie and launch the site on the internet. They would also manage all the subscribers; create a CD, a book and a guidance deck. Their price was ten thousand dollars for this service. WOW, I told Peter I would need to think about this.

In light of this new possible development on the horizon for the Morning Messages, I did not sleep much that night. I talked to the 'team' and they responded *"We say hooray, it has been great fun in the arrangement of this unfolding and this weaving. We will say there has been a certain level of resistance within you that has been present. However we are pleased that you have shifted that in order for this reality to come present."*

The rest of the night I pondered how I might come up that that amount of money. The next day I called a dear friend in Portland who was one of the few who knew the about the messages and told her of the offer. She was thrilled, and so supportive of this opportunity, she was willing to gift the project two thousand dollars. I called two other close friends and shared this news and each one stated they were in this game for a thousand dollars. I was filled with gratitude and amazement, there was a divine flow happening with these events, the incredible evidence of synchronicity working at its best. I contacted Peter and said, "I have raised four thousand dollars within 24 hours and I want to partner with your company, Pass Along Concepts." Astonished and amazed, I realized the 'team' had supported all these miraculous arrangements.

Once this commitment was made, it became an exciting whirlwind of activities. The 'team' invited me to find the pen and ink drawings that I had created with my left hand years ago. They stated that they had offered the energy for these drawings when that was what I could accept. These sketch books had been stored for over thirty years, and now in a few short days, were being scanned into the computer and numbered for reference. With the support of my friend LeAnn, we began to review the two hundred transmissions and select and edit the first forty-four messages that would be available on the new website. I signed the contract and arranged to bring all my material to the Pass Along Concept offices in Oregon to create the project.

Everything was flowing with such ease, it was amazing. Packed and ready with scripts, drawings and much enthusiasm, I flew to Ashland. Peter offered me the use of his apartment, and it was arranged for someone to pick me up each day and take me to the production site and offices. It was thrilling to work with this delightful staff of creative individuals. The design and look of the website was a top priority. Michael was my graphic artist, and together with his expertise and my 'team's' guidance, we created the brand, the look and the heading. It was an interesting experience for me to stand between these two realities. The 'team' was guiding me with the selection of images, the feel and the look, and Michael was skilled and willing to put the ideas into place.

The next day, I recorded the audio of the first transmission for the Flash movie. Robert had set the simple recorder on a desk, gave me instructions, and I was on my own. As I began to read this first transmission, I recognized the familiar feeling of the 'team's' presence, so my words were being infused with their energy. Once this was completed, the rest of the morning was spent with me selecting the images that would go with the forty-four messages.

Next was the creation of the Flash movie. I joined Travor, another creative individual, and we played with my audio script and our imagination. The 'team' was active in the selection and the look of the entire presentation. I would be sitting beside Travor with all his equipment and hear the 'team's' comment or delight with what we were creating. It was an incredible experience, a bit surreal.

All the basics were in place; now Robert, the owner of the company, would create the entire website. Unfortunately, he was flying to Turkey; and to meet the timeline that the 'team' had requested, he was planning to work on my project while there for holiday. The launch date had been selected because the 'team' was clear in communicating that there was an energetic portal opening which was a perfect opportunity to empower the launch of the messages. This world of technology was truly amazing and mystifying for this sixty-three year old woman, and so was the mystery of energetic portal openings.

When I returned home, a dear friend asked if I had received the other six thousand dollars. She suggested that I invite my friends to participate with the project and make a donation. I would then list them as sponsors on the website and they could ride this global wave with me. She also generously offered to contribute whatever amount was needed to meet the final financial goal. It was through the incredible support of my friends and community that the rest of the money was generated for the project. My basket of miracles was overflowing.

When they were ready to launch the website, www. morningmessages.com, with an invitation to thousands to subscribe to the forty-four free messages, the creative crew from Ashland called and began to count down, "... four-three-two-one, and send!" I felt this incredible rush of excitement. That moment, the very moment that we launched the project across the ether and onto the internet, my front door blew open. It was amazing timing. I was covered with chills as I realized it was the energy of my 'team' acknowledging what had just taken place. When I made contact they stated *"We desired to acknowledge you and the physical team that has brought this into form, opening the door was simply a symbolic way for us to state what had just happened. There has been a door opened for you and for others who will receive our messages. You could call this the 'open door project', and that would be true. This offering that you have anchored goes forth in ever increasing circles of hearts and minds. It has begun and will continue to expand. We embrace you with our gratitude."*

I woke the next morning absolutely terrified and nauseated. I immediately asked the 'team' "What is this about?" *"We address the issues of your fear, because it is fear that most starhumans carry. This is the old paradigm that you are being asked to address and invite others to shift as well. Your fears are patterns that keep you locked*

26

into the limited realms of your beliefs and programs. Remember when you consciously expand into a new space whatever fears or issues you carry will match the expansion." Oh... I then realized one of the issues of my entire life was that I was different and looked at life differently than most people. I had always felt a bit out of place, and here I have just stretched into the global community offering channeled transmissions. Talk about putting yourself on the line in a big way. With this awareness and understanding I took a big sigh and faced my fears once again — the terror and nausea disappeared.

Within a month, there were close to a thousand subscribers. The thrill of connecting with so many wonderful individuals was incredible. The e-mails began to pour in; the messages were touching the hearts and minds of the readers. They were remembering who they were, as magnificent multidimensional beings of love and light.

Soon after the launch, I received an e-mail which stated: "Peggy Black's Morning Messages web site was awarded the Reality Shifting Award of Excellence. The Reality Shifting Award of Excellence is given to one web site each month, and was awarded to Morning Messages in the month of September 2006 for demonstrating excellence in content and design, while being informative and unique in helping people shift their reality in a positive direction." I am amazed how these messages are touching so many people; I am humbled and filled with gratitude.

As the first few months went by there were technical problems with the site, and there were many glitches with the way the messages looked. I felt the site had been created in haste and there were mistakes. I continued to ask Robert to please correct or fix these issues. Some were taken care of and others were not. Each time I had an upset with the situation the 'team' would say *"All is well."* I would then relax into the events.

One day I received an e-mail invitation to join the Ocean of Gratitude with Dr. Emoto. Of course I accepted this wonderful opportunity from Karol who loved the Morning Messages and was arranging all details for this cruise. We spoke, and she invited me to offer a service while on the cruise. I shared that I could offer Sound Healing; she replied "We have someone who is offering Sound Healing." I could offer Reflexology; she replied "We have someone who is offering Reflexology." I heard the 'team' say *"Tell her you can offer channeled transmissions."* I actually heard myself say "I can offer channeled transmissions." "Excellent, write a paragraph for the program and send it to me as soon as possible." I was a bit stunned that I had just made that commitment.

I was also invited to bring water from my fountain of Waters of the World. This was water gathered at sacred wells, rivers, and sites from over three hundred locations around the world, each source retaining and yet contributing its own unique energy to the whole.

It would be an honor to share this energy of the Waters of the World and assist with the sacred water ceremony for the Ocean of Gratitude cruise. So I flew to Florida, joined two hundred like-minded individuals for this cruise, offering channeled transmissions; and I had never done one. For me it was a stretch, a really big stretch into a new level of trust. However I trusted the support of my 'team.' Once on the ship, I found a small room by the chapel which would serve as a private space for the appointments. My scheduled time was totally booked. At my first appointment, I sat in front of my client, offered an anchoring and a prayer and then asked my 'team' what do I do next? They replied *"Ask their full name, which gives us a focus."* It was amazing how it unfolded; information just flowed, yet I had no way of explaining how it happened.

A friend of mine was always saying to watch for signs along the way to assure yourself that you are on your path. Well, this trip certainly offered me signs. A group of us were getting on the elevator one afternoon when an employee of the cruise line stepped up and asked "Is there a Peggy here?" "Yes," I answered, and she stated "I am on my break and would like a reading if possible." I was stunned; I invited her into the elevator and asked how she knew about my readings. She had found one of our Ocean of Gratitude programs, and out of the several thousand people on the cruise, she had found me with absolute guidance. This entire cruise proved to be incredible, filled with amazing connections and synchronicities, as well as meeting and enjoying awesome people. I had once again trusted, and stretched into another expansion.

Once home again, back into the routine of answering e-mails and tending the garden, the 'team' invited me to announce to my morning message family that personal channeled transmissions were available. I still resisted. I spoke to my daughters who encouraged me and also made me aware that I would need to create CD's of the readings. This was far too technical for me to deal with. The 'team' continued to invite me to offer the channeled transmissions. I continued to resist, stating if they wanted me to do these readings they would have to provide a simple, easy way for me to record them. It was actually a few days later when I received an e-mail promoting accessories for the computer. I checked out the site, and wouldn't you know it, there was a piece of equipment called a USB recorder which connects to a phone and then records the conversation into an audio file on the computer. Unbelievable.

With gratitude I acknowledged another example of divine flow and support. Well needless to say, I ordered the USB recorder and had my entire office updated, installing a dedicated phone line for the channeled readings. An account with PayPal was established, making it easy for the financial exchange. Thank goodness for the skills and guidance of others who appeared like magic when needed, who willingly supported me along these learning curves and these stretches into the world of cyber space. Up to this point in my life I had actually been more comfortable with exploring inner space.

I finally announced this opportunity to others, that they could receive a personal channeled transmission with the 'team.' Another incredible door opened. I began to connect with individuals from around the world, sharing the energy, guidance and love from 'the team.' I became the fair witness to these personal transmissions, trusting that when I created a safe space and relaxed there was a flow of energy and information. I had no real idea how this process worked, but the energy that would be present during these times was always precious and indescribable. There was a flow here that I recognized and honored. Though this connection was becoming more natural and constant, I was still amazed at what was occurring.

As I continued to embrace and be more comfortable in connecting with the divine consciousness, my 'team,' it become more and more evident to me that the non-physical beings of love and light wanted our partnership. With their guidance, I came to see that it was our birthright to connect with this divine energy and consciousness, and to become the conscious bridge between spirit and matter. When I allowed my connection with the 'team' to expand, offering personal channeled transmissions, information just flowed. At some point in the reading, the individual was encouraged to connect and begin a partnership with their own beloved team. I was curious and inquired about this, and was told that I was simply a liaison, introducing each client to their own divine connection. This connection is always made by our personal invitation allowing incredible love and support from the non-physical realms to become a part of our physical walk. It seems that it is our legacy, our privilege, and our birthright to interface with the loving non-physical divine consciousness. It is our honor to allow and anchor divine consciousness in this reality and timeframe.

On the physical aspect, I was still responsible to anchor this unfolding venture. Each time I inquired about creating the spoken word CD or beginning production of the Morning Messages book or guidance deck projects, I was put off by the company. This was a puzzle to me since we had an agreement and a contract, we were in a partnership. I was then reminded each time when I felt the disappointment that *"All is well."*

There was something happening within the company that was hosting the Morning Messages. I became aware that staff members were leaving and calls and e-mails were not being returned. Finally I was told that there was no money to create the book, the CD, or the guidance deck which I had been promised. The company was in financial trouble. When I learned this news, I was extremely upset. I remember hearing once again the phrase *"All is well."* I shouted "I want something MORE than all is well!" It was an hour or so later when I had relaxed a bit into this disappointment, when I heard *"All is well and MORE"* which made me laugh out loud. This phrase became my mantra in the days to come.

I was ready to take legal action over this issue, but finally decided it would be in my best interest and the best interest of Morning Messages to practice what the 'team' encouraged, and to find a more peaceful solution. My contract was ended with Pass Along Concepts and was resolved as best as was possible at the time. I now owned my website and my list of subscribers, with the agreement of six future e-mail blasts and two hundred posters to be printed. I felt like this business partnership had failed. In one of my morning sessions with the 'team' I inquired as to why this had happened. I was told:

"This vehicle, this program was the quickest manner we could get the messages launched. We feel it was very successful, the goal was accomplished. You held a clear space of integrity from your authentic Self that was a huge learning and growth for you. Now look within and see what characteristics the other person has that you dislike or disapprove of, what activates you? These are yours, hidden in the deep unconsciousness of your psyche. They are like prisoners. It is time to free and forgive them. Acknowledge the benefits of this experience. Remember a few months ago very few selected people knew of the messages, now there are several thousand who have been exposed to our words. We applaud your willingness to anchor this energy and bring it forth. We applaud your tenacity in holding the vision. We are always delighted to touch this same space with you. We encourage you to step into your joy and gratitude. This is one of the biggest lessons and biggest challenges for you and most humans."

Needless to say, the next few months were challenging and frustrating. I was quickly thrust into the world of technology. I became responsible for the entire Morning Messages website and all that was involved. I shifted all the underpinnings of this project, opening my own hosting account and moving the entire website as well as the list of two thousand subscribers. Learning a new language with new words of systems, access codes, outputs, megabytes, gigabytes, databases, log me in's, and back me up's. The universe provided me with a web wizard named Datta who became my guide and the translator in this strange non-physical terrain of cyber space and the internet. He held my virtual hand so to speak and made all these changes possible.

One of the most important aspects of this phase of the project was to have the presentation of the messages redesigned and the website errors corrected. A new set of forty-four messages was selected to be offered. This process itself took several weeks since they were chosen from the over two hundred transmissions stored in my computer. They were edited and formatted and the website was programmed to offer this next set of free messages. I was now stepping into this role and embracing not only the spiritual space where I connected with the 'team' but this virtual world of electronic communications where I was connecting with hearts and minds of so many special individuals. These connections were the true miracles.

Each time a trial or a test of my knowledge of this new electronic world surfaced, my mantra was *"All is well and more."* All these changes and upgrades that were taking place with the Morning Messages project and website were costly and the funds were coming from my savings, yet there was no doubt that this was the right thing to do.

Everything with the shift in the website, the redesigned look of the messages, the beginning of monthly newsletters, was all going well. Now as the owner of this project I also discovered that there were hundreds of unanswered e-mails being held on the site. I had not recognized this source of incoming mail from the many wonderful individuals who had been receiving the messages. Ooops. Oh my! Slowly, I began to answer these acknowledgments, realizing that the Morning Messages were making much more of an impact on the readers than I could imagine. The sharing was heart opening, heart warming and certainly encouraging when I was feeling a bit challenged or discouraged.

During this entire time in which the Morning Messages project was taking place, I was still active with all the usual daily responsibilities, as well as teaching monthly workshops, hosting several monthly groups in my home and traveling to various conferences and events. Also added to the schedule were monthly free audio webcasts. All the details and the technical skills were handled by my friend Randy; I would just call in and be connected with the morning message family all over the world. What a joy and a thrill to share the 'team' and offer a live transmission. This new stretch opened many doors and invitations for interviews and a number of blog radio programs. Needless to say, this was an extremely active time in my life, exciting, full, rich, and yet incredibly busy.

Weaving my other activities with these new responsibilities, the days generated their own rhythms and I settled into the new pace of rising early, answering e-mails, conducting the business and offering appointments for the channeled transmissions. The 'team' began to invite me to make a CD of the messages. This invitation continued for a number of weeks. Since I was now responsible for the cost of creating the CD, I finally said to the 'team', "When you find a recording studio that is close to my home, and inexpensive, I will make the CD; until then, don't ask again."

A number of days went by and I contacted a friend whom I had known for over thirty years who had lived a quarter mile from my home. He had just moved and I wanted to find out how he was doing. In our conversation, I remembered a mutual friend that I had not thought of in years, so I asked him if he was still in touch with Brian. He shared that Brian and his wife had actually bought his house before he moved to Palm Springs. My next and most important question was "Does Brian still have a recording studio?" The reply was, "Yes, I believe it is in the spare room." Of course I acquired the phone number and called Brian as soon as possible. He was delighted to hear from me and willing to assist me with the CD project. Adding another miracle to this list, it just happened that his specialty was editing spoken word CDs.

The ease of this unfolding was amazing; I acknowledged this remarkable manifestation and support from the 'team.' There was no question, I would keep my agreement and create the CD. We scheduled two recording times and I took the script for the first forty-four messages from the website. Brian's recording studio was compact, filled with all this intriguing equipment and several computer screens. Once I had recorded the messages, Brian worked his magic and created an audio version of the Morning Messages. In the meantime, I was also working with my graphic artist, Melanie, to design the cover. This was the exciting and fun part. I contacted a company who would take the master files of spoken words and create the CD. Brian began editing my recorded words and creating the master file. This was the first time he had ever heard the messages. He had to listen to them repeatedly as he was editing, which apparently took long hours because of my vocal errors and breathiness.

He shared with me a dilemma he experienced — apparently as he observed and edited the waveform of my voice, there was another interesting wave pattern which showed up on his screen. At first he thought something might be wrong with the equipment, however he soon realized what he was witnessing was the energy transmission from the 'team' being woven into the energy field of my voice. He was surprisingly generous with his time and the costs of his expertise, sharing with me how important he felt these messages were to the world. The 'team' had answered my request of a studio close to home and inexpensive. They had provided the connection with this most ideal and talented person who was touched by their mission and service. The synchronicity of this unfolding was delicious.

Two weeks later, several boxes of beautiful CDs arrived; I sat on the floor and wept. I heard the 'team' say *"If the other company had made the CDs, they would not have carried our energy transmission. All is well and more; we are pleased."* This CD experience offered awareness and a lesson for me—to realize that sometimes, when things do not seem to work out the way I had hoped or planned, there was actually a more fulfilling outcome in the future. This lesson continued to show up in my life with other projects, always inviting me to stretch into trust.

According to our agreement, Robert sent an e-blast to his large list of internet members and the result was wonderful. The CDs "We Are Here" Transmissions, the Morning Messages had been launched. My inbox of e-mails was flooded with new enrollments and orders. Now there was an audio of the messages and transmissions which carried an energy of transformation to all those who listened.

To celebrate the creation of the CD, I arranged an evening event at Gateways, the local metaphysical bookstore. My excitement level was a ten as this was my favorite store, and they were hosting my gathering. Imagine that. It was a wonderful group of dear friends and community coming together to celebrate with me. A friend offered to make a video of the evening. The joy for me was sharing my connection with my 'team,' this loving celestial consciousness and all the miracles, blessings and synchronicities that had unfolded with our partnership. The evening was rich.

Within days there was an invitation to create a DVD of the evening and the sharing. I contacted Brian and he agreed to edit the film; Melanie and I designed the entire package, and it was a go. Brian discovered that the footage needed much editing because of camera movement. I had to decide if it was a yes or no. I was told by the 'team' that the DVD also carried a transmission of energy and was important. So it was a yes.

Brian was a wizard with his editing. What a whirlwind; I was traveling and needed to approve the proofs on a computer in a hotel, not an easy task. When my stress level was high, I heard *"All is well and more,"* which was always an invitation to take a breath, sigh and find my gratitude. This pause of gratitude consistently allowed a shift. I realized that I was moving between the dimensions, operating in ordinary day to day three dimensional activities, as well as bringing in the energy and transmissions from the higher dimensions, weaving them together and then supporting their physical manifestation and creation.

I was a bridge between the physical and the non-physical. I remember when this all began and the 'team' called me their transducer. I had no idea what a transducer was. It certainly didn't sound like a nice title or one that would fit in my resume. It was months later that I discovered the meaning; a transducer is a speaker or amplifier that receives energy from one system and retransmits it in a different form into another system. So I claimed the role as transducer, scribe and witness. The 'team' had also shared with me in the beginning, hoping to offer me clarification of our partnered relationship, *"We are woven into the fabric of your energetic signature. We are your wave link and you are our focus. Be at peace beloved and know that you are loved and supported."*

I honored my role as the active partner in this physical dimension and continued to move our projects forward. This work/service had become my everyday activity. I remember a few years ago I would call my young grandson whenever I got lost on the computer. So this was a real expansion for me; constantly learning new computer skills, business skills, making decisions and setting up a strong business support. As the CD was being created I realized that I would need professional assistance with the orders, so I found a wonderful fulfillment company in the Midwest. My computer wizard designed the product page and the shopping cart features for the website; more decisions, more computer speak, more systems to integrate and new passwords to select. The only password needed for any shift in consciousness is gratitude, but in the electronic realms it's a different story.

Everything that was created or offered in the Morning Messages project had so many multi-levels and dimensions. The physical aspect had the most details, all of which seemed to be sent by attachments, PDFs, e-mails and such. It was amazing to me that I now had a number of talented individuals assisting with all these projects that I had never physically met; they lived all across the country and they were young enough to be my grandchildren. This virtual world was as mysterious and amazing as any of the worlds I travel.

The CDs of the messages and the DVDs were finally complete and available. The website was up to date, the fulfillment company had product. There was a pause as the holidays were happening and the family traditions were occurring once again. Life was good and life was blessed. I was so grateful for the wonder of all that I was witnessing. I stepped into the New Year and all the awesome surprises and gifts that it offered. The appointments for channeled transmissions were booked, orders were placed. I was the witness to this awesome transformation in my life, being totally supported by such loving, clear energy. The feelings are ineffable, witnessing the abundance of the miracles and synchronicities.

Foolish of me to think that I could rest on these successes, the 'team' invites me to create the Morning Messages deck of guidance cards. So once again I began sifting through the files, three pages for each transmission, selecting the suggestions offered by the 'team.' These exercises were intended to shift or expand one's perspective. These invitations were mental and emotional tools which allowed a new viewpoint of reality and would empower the individual to remember their magnificence.

This process took many months of honing the words of the 'team' into a very concise offering for each card. My dear friend Jennifer would join me once a week and we would read and re-read each card distilling the message to under a hundred and forty words. It was an interesting process because the original transmission could be over a thousand words. I was just selecting the practices of expanded consciousness that the 'team' had offered in the context of the entire transmission.

As I selected, edited and prepared the contents for the deck I was also busy researching to find a company who would produce them for me. I soon discovered that the making of a guidance deck was very costly; each card would be printed in color on both sides, as well as coated with a protective sealant which takes a special piece of equipment. How to present the deck was also a consideration, what kind of box or container would be the best and the most cost effective? Most of the printing companies in the United States who had the necessary equipment to create this product were over the top expensive. I talked to the 'team' and asked for their support in this search. Amazingly, the next day I received the name of a representative of a company in China which could and would produce the deck at a reasonable price. This project was truly going global.

The forty-four messages were edited and ready. One morning I sat with all the messages and all the stick drawings, and together with the 'team' selected and matched the illustration with the message on each card. When I asked the 'team', "Do I call these guidance cards or oracle cards," I was told, *"They are invitations to practice a consciousness exercise which empowers and honors our magnificent multidimensional Starself."* They were tools to support an individual to stay in a coherent vibration of joy, gratitude and appreciation. So the deck officially became the Morning Messages Invitations.

One of the most exciting aspects of this experience was sitting next to my graphic artist friend Melanie, speaking the same creative language and actually creating the deck. She had the computer skills and programs which allowed us to design each card. The Orion nebula was the background for the CD cover, so it felt perfect to use this stunning galactic image for the back of each card. The idea was that you could lay out the cards side by side and the entire nebula would be re-created. It was a visual and energetic matrix.

Even though this process was fun and satisfying, it was also very time-consuming and rather tedious. We were working in a specific energy portal. We had sixteen powerful days which would infuse this work with awesome galactic energy. In partnership with the creative process came the left brain details with the printing company in China, the contract, pricing and timelines. The requirements were extremely detailed with scores of pages that required many files to be set up. Working with Vickie, the representative in Portland, was tedious: I would ask my question, and then she would contact the office in China, and there was always a day or two delay just because of the time difference. My intention was to have the decks complete and ready by the holidays. And this was August— however, I was aware that I was working with an energy which continues to bless the projects with extraordinary miracles and support. So I continued to practice relaxing into trust for the perfect outcome, and sometimes this was literally a moment to moment exercise.

Melanie and I started our creative process the first day of the energy portal, and we worked several hours every day for the next sixteen days. My excitement level continued to increase as I watched the unfolding of this vision, and I began to see the results of the previous eight months. Time was of an essence, especially because we were working globally. We had to send the files to China for a color test; they printed our images and sent the actual proofs by snail mail. Once they received our entire PDF file, it would take over two months for the three thousand Morning Messages Invitation decks to be created and delivered to the ship in China, sail across the ocean and then move by truck to the fulfillment company here in the United States. There were lots of stages and steps to be coordinated and integrated on the physical plane.

The excitement of the project kept me going during the day. At night, however, I would wake up and wonder just how I was going to generate the $10,000 to cover all the costs. I did not have enough in savings, or in any other account. What could I sell; what could I do? After several nights of this kind of pondering and worrying, I simply said to the 'team', "You have to assist me with the finances." Just before falling sleep, I heard *"Invite the readers to be a part of this manifestation."* The next day, I composed a letter which invited one hundred Morning Messages readers to sponsor this project by paying one hundred dollars in advance for ten decks delivered before the holidays. This letter was sent out to the subscribers and the response was phenomenal—within the month the entire ten thousand dollars had been generated. My heart swelled with gratitude as I opened a dedicated holding account at my bank. It was a miracle, an absolute miracle, and another lesson of trust for me. Anchor the vision, infuse it with passion, take action, and trust that the support will manifest.

The company had sent me several samples of boxes for the cards. Of course I loved the most expensive box; it was easy to open and felt comfortable in my hand. The other boxes did not open well and were fragile. Here was the tricky part: Melanie and I had to design the graphic for this box, which had twelve separate surfaces. We needed to make sure that the text and graphics were in the proper place and going in the correct direction when it was printed and wrapped on the box. Let me tell you this was a process. Melanie would set it up and print the one piece wrap and I would cut it out and proceed to try it on our sample box, which had been custom made just for this deck.

The color proofs from China arrived in the mail and did not meet my expectations; the colors seemed dull. Oh my, what to do? I was fully committed at this point to complete this project on time and honor all the sponsors. I realized that I needed to begin to sculpt the energy surrounding this project and the results. Knowing the power of the spoken word infused with clear focused emotions, I called my intention partners Ellen and Suzanna for assistance. We have been witnessing and supporting one another's intentions for over a decade with phenomenal results. Ellen and I set up the framework of the entire creative process of the Morning Messages Invitation deck. We began with the completed PDF's of the graphics and followed through step by step until the invitation decks were delivered to the sponsors.

Here are some examples of the intentions we crafted: It is my intention the entire master set of graphics arrive safely at the printers; It is my intention that the files can be opened easily; It is my intention that the printing equipment operates at its best; It is my intention that the staff printing the deck is highly qualified and experienced; It is my intention that the colors used result in brilliant reproductions of the graphics; It is my intention that every aspect of the creation of this deck is supervised by the 'team' so that the quality is excellent; We literally took this step by step, considering every phase and aspect, working with the energetic field of infinite possibilities, holding the focus clearly, holding the vision of what was desired and calling the best results forward.

And we covered both sides of the ocean with our anticipatory gratitudes as well as our intentions. For example: I am grateful that the roads are clear and the delivery trucks operate smoothly; I am grateful that the ship carrying the boxes of finished product has excellent weather and arrives on time; I am grateful that everyone who touches this project in any way is blessed; I believe you get the idea. We engaged the quantum field, we saw the end results, and we envisioned and held the energetic framework in place. Once this was completed, with our energetic framework in place, over the next few months I would call Suzanna to reinforce these intentions, especially when I would get squirrelly with some worry or concern. It was a constant reset and a very powerful learning to surrender.

As another lesson in trust, I approved of the less than perfect color proofs and held the vision and intention that what I desired would be created. Melanie and I finished up all the graphics, meeting all the requirements from the printer. We packaged up everything, the PDFs, the printed samples of each page, clear directions and our intentions and prayers. I literally raced to the FedEx service with only minutes to spare in order to send these master files to China on the last day of the powerful portal we had been working within.

My drive home was emotional; I was grateful, relieved and excited. This had been an eight month process, escalating to hyper-speed these last sixteen days. In two months, the final phase of printing and packaging would be complete. Everything must go incredibly smoothly; our timeline window was extremely tight, each day was important to the success and timely delivery. Expect the unexpected with grace, however. The package arrived in China, but the production plant was closed for a three day holiday. It felt like our timeline was already three days late. More intentions and more prayers; the 'team' assures me *"All is well and more."*

Back to the routine of juggling my time with appointments, house and garden care, office tasks and other responsibilities. The days were richly filled with the flow of my regular life's activities, and the monthly gathering for Sound Pod and the women's support group Miracles, Intentions and Prayers which has been meeting once a month for sixteen years. This group energy has witnessed, supported and held my intentions through many changes, transformations and much growth, blessing my life in amazing ways.

As the weeks went by filled with the daily endeavors, always in the back of my mind were thoughts about the deck. Finally a small package arrived from China. My hands trembled as I began to open the wrappings; it was the finished product of the entire deck, the proofs, which had to be approved before they printed the three thousand others. When I realized I was holding my breath, I stopped opening the package; I sighed and placed my awareness in my heart, generating feelings of gratitude and joy. Once I was centered in my heart space of gratitude, I continued. When I removed the last of the wrappings, there was the Morning Messages Invitation deck, glowing in all its beauty, grace and energy. It was perfect. The box that cradled the cards was beyond my expectation and intentions, each card stunning with brilliantly alive colors.

Every aspect was how I had envisioned it. I fanned out all the cards, I touched each one; I wept, I danced, I shouted and I gave thanks at the top of my lungs for the impressive support from the physical and the non-physical teams that had empowered this awesome creation.

My approval was instantly communicated to China; the rest of this process was a piece of cake. In the framework of the intentions, the clear focused energy and gratitude, the rest of the project was completed in perfect timing. Even though there was severe weather and various other possible blockages that could have delayed delivery, the focus, the intentions and prayers of the many supporters allowed the finished Morning Messages Invitation decks to move with ease and grace into reality.

I was on a cloud, feeling such joy and appreciation. I felt incredibly connected to the whole divine community, bridging the physical and the non-physical. Recognizing the amazing unfolding of these last couple of years and all that had manifested and truly transformed my life. Each step unfolded surrounded by awesome miracles, blessings and synchronicities. I continued to shift each disappointment or challenge by striving to stay in a frequency of gratitude and deep appreciation.

Several hundred beautiful finished decks arrived, via air, at my home, just in time for a conference. The remaining decks were on a ship somewhere in the middle of the ocean, not due at the fulfillment company for several more weeks. Packed and ready, travel plans continued and the decks were presented with great success at the four day event. The rest of the year was a whirlwind of appointments, more travel, excitements and acknowledgments from the sponsors who finally received their ten decks in time for the holidays. Wow, what an exciting and fulfilling year—I had even added another free monthly audio webcast hosted by my new friend Cyndi. This work/service was expanding beyond my wildest dreams.

The New Year began with a full calendar of travel plans including another Ocean of Gratitude cruise in March. In January, however, it was off to Kauai to see family and for the Wellness Expo. My family visit was emotional and a bit tense; and the expo was slow because of the economy. Home to unpack, settle in and handle all the other tasks and responsibilities, I was excited about all the new possibilities unfolding. My life and projects were moving forward in a graceful and smooth manner.

Then life shifted very quickly with a middle of the night emergency call from my daughter. She needed help! I was packed again and on a plane within hours, returning to Kauai. Everything was arranged and ten days later she was in a recovery program in southern California. I returned home concerned and shaken. It was important that I get ready and repack for the cruise. I flew to Florida, joined the others, and realized just how exhausted I was as I retreated into my stateroom and slept. The cruise was a bit of a blur of people and noise as my focus and prayers were with my daughter. After one quick night at home, I collected my pre-packed luggage and returned to the airport to fly down south to see my daughter and be a part of her program. Once home again, I received news that my eldest daughter was also going through a crisis, with her job and the end of her marriage. Looking back, I am not sure just how I was able to manage all that. However, we each rally when it is necessary.

I had shared with my morning message family the life changes and challenges my daughters were experiencing. I knew that my sharing would resonate with many who were encountering similar circumstances with their loved ones. The response was inspiring. I received a flood of supportive e-mails, including stories of what others were personally going through with their family and the challenges they were courageously embracing.

I took to heart the messages from the 'team' to see the best for each beloved daughter and to hold the vision and the emotion of their well-being and the perfect outcome for the experience. My dear friend Barbara shared one of her teachings with me — it was a simple exercise to say, "I am grateful. I am grateful. I am grateful." With every beat of my heart and every breath that I take, I am grateful." I would say that several times then I would make a grateful statement for the situation with each daughter: "I am grateful that _ _____ finds the perfect job. I am grateful for the perfect solution to _____.   I am grateful that this _____ issue has been resolved in the most supportive manner."

My personal shifting of how I was thinking about my loved ones assisted in the transformation of my reality and how I was holding the situation. When a worry thought arose, I tossed it out as quickly as possible and replaced it with a thought/emotion that was uplifting. Frequently this was a moment to moment exercise. However it became easier with practice. The prayers of support and kind letters became my foundation as they supported me with such love. We are all facing tremendous challenges of change and the support of one another is what gives us the courage to call forth the future we long to embrace.

I was told that I needed to take it easy since it seems my adrenals were a bit overworked. Imagine that. All the plans for more travel, workshops and promotion of the Morning Messages products were put on hold. I softened my days. I began to sleep in and rest in the afternoon. Seems the exciting push and the intensity of taking over the website, handling all the e-mails and engaging in creating the three products one after the other had taken their toll. The days took on a gentler rhythm. I continued to offer appointments for personal readings and allow myself grace concerning my usual intense days. I hired a wonderful office goddess, Nicole who assisted me with all the paper work. I began to heal and my daughters began to heal. I was grateful for support, prayers and blessings from my family, community, and my morning messages family, which meant a lot to me during those days. There were times when I could literally feel the embrace of this energy.

In sharing my challenges during the year, others identified with me. I continued to receive an outpouring of e-mails from people around the globe sharing their stories and their personal challenges. It felt like a hard year, with all that my daughters were going through, several close relationships that shifted, and several dear friends who passed away. I experienced a number of significant disappointments concerning the Morning Messages products—the main one was the New Age Trade show in Denver. Despite the Morning Messages website being awarded the 2009 Coalition of Visionary Resources Visionary Award of Excellence, the show did not result in the phenomenal success and sales I had anticipated. It was an expensive week too; the costs had doubled since I had taken my office goddess along. I returned home and retreated.

During all these events and disappointments, I received support and encouragement from my beloved 'team' and continued to share their wisdom and guidance with others through the monthly newsletters and the appointments for personal transmissions. Some days staying centered happened breath to breath. I was continually reframing the events and looking for the benefits, remembering how important my state of mind and my personal vibrations were in shifting the experience. I was encouraged to realize that each of these experiences had offered me the opportunity to step into my grace, to shift my perspective, and find and anchor my gratitude. Remembering that we are divine and here to transform dysfunctional energy is one of our assignments as the magnificent multidimensional beings that we are.

The personal readings that were given each month allowed me to realize how individuals were also dealing with these personal, global and evolutionary shifts. The challenges they were facing in job losses, health issues and family crises were humbling. I was continually inspired by their courage, and willingness to uplift and consciously deal with these tragedies. The 'team' constantly reminded each one of their personal power and their true ability to shift any dysfunctional energy in their life, repeatedly sharing that we are a part of the collective matrix, and when one was uplifted and healed, all were uplifted and healed.

When emotions are intense, and there's an overwhelming feeling of fear or depression, the first thing to ask is "What percent of these emotions are personally mine and what percent belongs to the collective?" We are all a part of this energy field, this quantum field of energy, this collective matrix. The service that we can offer each day is to shift our own personal vibrations, our personal energy, and by doing so we affect the collective every time. We are all one. We are energy transformers pure and simple. If it is before us, it is there to be healed, transformed and uplifted.

In the fall, I received a clear message from the 'team' to offer a special invitation to others to participate during the powerful energetic portal of 09-09-09. They offered the script early one morning during our session. It was called "A Call to Action for Lightworkers, Help Cleanse the Currency." I shared this idea and invitation with my friend Amrita and she immediately said, "This needs to be on YouTube!" At first I resisted, but she assured me that we could do it and offer it in time.

We set up the process and then realized that her audio recorder didn't record very well. New tactic: I would read directly into the computer—we actually went into my closet in order to buffer the other noises. She then took the recording and created the video. I shared the text with another friend, and he said the title was too long and not strong enough. I told him the YouTube video was finished, but he offered to pay for the remake titled simply "Cleanse the Currency." A new video was made and launched on the internet. The results were phenomenal.

My e-mails reached several hundred very quickly. This was activating everyone. This simple YouTube video went "spiral" (I know, I know, but 'viral' just bothers my sense of the positive!) all over the globe, on other websites, on Facebook, and blogs. Thousands upon thousands of people were sharing this invitation to "Cleanse the Currency." I was invited to be on a number of web radio programs. I was amazed and stunned. The 'team' encouraged everyone to be conscious when currency passed through our hands with all the financial exchanges, to bless and energetically clear the money of any vibration of fear, lack, or scarcity. Once again the 'team' had offered a suggestion which inspired and empowered others to transform the dysfunctional energy around money.

September 10th, I had a phone appointment with a publisher, who I was hoping would publish the Morning Messages. She inquired what I was doing, and in my excitement I shared the "Cleanse the Currency" project and the astounding success. This was the book she wanted, could I give her more suggestions about how to work with energy in our daily activities. Without hesitation I said yes. I spent the next few days writing and composing these suggestions; I also included some of the original transmissions from the 'team' that offer ways to transform energy. Unfortunately, she felt there were two voices speaking and she did not want the channeled voice. She was still interested if I could give her twenty five thousand words in my voice, offering basic energy exercises.

So I made a commitment with myself and dedicated the next month to writing a thousand words a day. I called upon all my past experiences and knowledge of working with energy. The title could have been "Energy Work 101" with chapters on the Energy Matrix, Traffic Matrix, Hospital Matrix, Conscious Interface, Energy Hygiene, and Body Talk. When I had twenty five thousand, one hundred and eleven words, I celebrated and I sent them off. Now I was filled with waiting, excited and thrilled with the opportunity.

The activities of my days were smooth, my daughters were doing well, client appointments continued to come in. Life was good; the pace was busy yet regular, as the holidays approached. Then, another assignment. I heard *"Heal the Healthcare, use the energy portal of 11-11-2009."* That was less than two weeks away, so I decided I would pass on that suggestion, or so I thought. "Heal the Healthcare" — those words were continuously streaming into my mind. Finally, in the middle of the night, unable to sleep, I agreed to take action. The next morning I spoke to my friend Amrita and told her we needed to make a new YouTube video. The same process occurred, and it was launched within a couple of days. The response was not as electric as "Cleanse the Currency" which activated everyone. However the 'team' assured me that our effort had added to the collective.

My time shifts to family and the upcoming holidays and celebrations. I find myself withdrawn and inward as I make the preparations, desiring quiet alone time to recharge and renew, wanting to shift any energy or emotions I was still holding and heal the perceived painful events of this past year. I was able to do this work in small segments; however, I knew there was more to be released and transformed. I was ready to release and heal all the imagined losses and disappointments. The weeks from Thanksgiving to New Years were always especially busy and active with people. I did my best to be prepared for these intense times. I love the holidays, yet as a sensitive, they can be a bit overwhelming.

I had long been aware that I was a bit of a recluse, living surrounded by nature in the redwoods for the last thirty-five years. The freeway was only four miles away, yet it did not interfere with the deer in the meadow, nor the covey of quail that cluck together eating the birdseed. My days were inlaid with these moments of unexpected delight, connecting with the beauty and wonder of this world. My days usually start by honoring the dawn, watching the sky herald a new beginning. The unfolding of the days are rich and full as I weave the threads of my desk work and appointments with the magical threads of interfacing with nature, knowing that I am truly blessed.

The New Year was celebrated with an open house and labyrinth walk which honored our intentions of wholeness; this has been a tradition since the beginning of this century. It was 1999 when the 'team' invited me to create a labyrinth in the garden to be available as an energy portal. I was told it was a dimensional doorway. Each year since 2000, the labyrinth has anchored energy for the shift of consciousness occurring within the collective matrix.

The labyrinth walk was followed a few days later by the celebration of my sixty-eighth year. Each birthday I take a dozen of my women friends to lunch, followed with a day of play, laughter, browsing downtown and catching a movie or two. Once all these holiday activities had occurred, I stepped back into my quiet zone, making a point and dedication of clearing out the old emotional baggage from last year using prayer, sounds and intentions. So January was spent as the opportunity to clear the past and visualize the coming year. Each time I released some old pattern or wound, it was replaced by a new dream supported by intentions and action.

February's schedule was resuming a natural rhythm as I awaited news of the possible book contract from the publisher. February was also another milestone — it had been five years since the first transmission and the beginning of this extraordinary journey. Looking back I was amazed by the wonderously unfolding events, all dovetailing in perfect synchronicity.

Astonished and humbled with the realization the messages have reached thousands and thousands of readers. I was grateful to have been in service as the witness, transducer and scribe to this loving conscious energy. This partnership with my 'team' had literally stretched and expanded me in every direction and dimension. I was as amazed by my new computer skills and use of the internet, as I was about the unfolding ability to offer personal channeled transmissions, both of which continue to remain a bit of a mystery; I am still uncertain of how they work.

Finally I received the news, the publisher declined the Cleanse the Currency manuscript. Shucks! I was disappointed and a bit surprised; I thought that the 'team' had been the source of this connection and the opportunity was a given. That night I tucked my disappointment around me like a blanket. Waking at dawn puzzled and frustrated, I went to the computer and made contact with the 'team'. The morning was as gray as my mood. I asked, "What happened here, I thought this was on open door?" The reply was: *"We are aware of the sense of disappointment about the news of the book; remember that there is more to be revealed. We invite you to step into your joy and express your gratitude even in this disappointment. The gifts of this experience will manifest in amazing ways, so hold the space for that to unfold. As you share with others, use your tools to transform this situation. We suggest that you prepare, get ready, and take action. We invite you to take action daily toward the goals that you desire. When you do this we are able to flow our energy into the action and support the results. Enough sleeping, enough waiting. CALL IT FORWARD. Spend quality time with us for your own personal connection and guidance. We are able to stream more fully when you are in your passion, holding the vision, and have made the time."*

"Right now, I am more aware of time than I have ever been in my life. I am beginning to look at the fact of my mortality, and the time left to do this work that you have invited me to do." *"We invite you to shift that perspective; and again we say GO FOR IT! If the passion is there, if the idea is there, a door will open for the results to occur. These are exciting days for you. You have the tools and the ability to create and serve. In partnership we will assist you in these physical manifestations; TRUST."* "I get caught up with the issue of finances and what I perceive as lack of funding." *"We are aware of this issue for you and continue to encourage you to TRUST."* At this point, I list all the projects for Morning Messages and I ask "Do you accept the invitation to support me financially with these projects?" *"We will support you. Step into your personal power. You are loved beyond measure. Be at peace beloved."*

Once this dialog was complete, the first inspiration that came to me was to take action in creating the Morning Messages "We Are Here" Transmissions book. This project had always been dear to my heart and had been a request of many of the subscribers and readers of the messages. When I opened the first e-mail that day there was a donation of one hundred dollars and an order for two hundred dollars and before noon four new appointments had been booked. Wow, that was quick support! I made a commitment with myself to get up before dawn and begin to share the story and the unfolding adventure of the miracles of the Morning Messages. The month of February was one of my most prosperous months for readings. The 'team' was keeping their agreements, and I was keeping my commitments as their scribe and their interface with this physical dimension.

The awareness of and relationship with my 'team' has been revealed gradually over my lifetime. I realize now that the left-handed drawings were yet another method used to illustrate our connection. I understand that the awesome and unusual sounds as well as the healing information for each client were also coming from my 'team.' Looking back, I can understand and recognize all the times I was receiving guidance and clear messages from this supportive and loving 'team.' They were connecting with me in as many ways as possible and in the ways I was willing and ready to accept. It has been a lifetime of gentle, loving, patient revealing.

In reviewing these last few years, I realize that perhaps my biggest expansion has been in the area of TRUST, taking each step, each day, each experience with wonder and gratitude. I continue learning to grab my fear before it grabs me, learning that "all is well and more," learning that there is always more to be revealed — which brings me back to TRUST. Learning to ask and allowing the support to show up, learning to be open for all possibilities, realizing and recognizing that I am a part of an amazingly complex and interrelated matrix of energy and consciousness. These all remain daily exercises of awareness, as does appreciating the incredible connection we each have to divine source and the all that is. The celestial realms of love and light are ever ready to assist us and come to our aid and support.

In fact, the celestial realm of Divine Essence and All That Is wants to be our active partner participating in our earthly journey. It is our birthright to be supported, guided and assisted by this divine energy. We are the bridge between spirit and matter, between heaven and earth. We are the open door which allows and invites divine consciousness into our reality, our challenges and our dreams. We were not meant to make this earthly sojourn alone; our own divine celestial self is meant to be in partnership with our celestial guides and teams, intertwined as an intimate active part of the matrix of divine consciousness.

Looking back gives one the opportunity to see things in a fresh and new way. From my perspective now, I can see the steps that led me to a conscious, aware connection with the loving energy group from another dimension that I call my 'team'. The Morning Messages transmissions that are being shared with thousands by means of the web site are now available in this book.

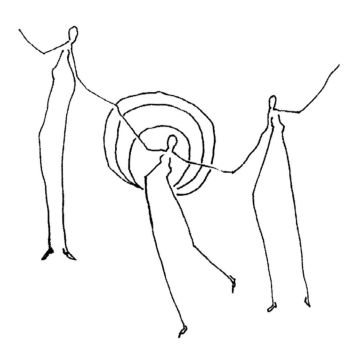

Opening the Door...

These eighty-eight Morning Messages will open new doors and bust down some of your old doors and beliefs. The Messages offer truths that will stretch your beliefs in a playful yet insightful manner. Each Message will intrigue and encourage you to practice fresh ways of looking at your life.

They will honor your magnificence and invite you to step into your power as a multidimensional being. They will challenge you to transform the difficulties in your daily life. They will inspire you to own the truth of who you really are. They will dare you to maintain an attitude of joy, gratitude and appreciation in the face of life changes. They will challenge you to play full out in your life, knowing that you make a difference.

You can drink them in slowly or in one quick fast gulp. It is recommended that you mentally sip them. Allow the ideas and suggestions to touch the taste buds of your mind and then explode in flavors of deliciously expanded concepts and realizations. These Messages will push against some of your most favorite and familiar mental foods.

The Morning Messages website offers these eighty-eight Messages free to subscribers. In four years this family of readers has grown close to 10,000 global members.

It is by request of these wonderful subscribers that this book has been created. The readers shared that they printed out the Messages so they could read them again and again. They created files, and they were upset when they missed a Message. The readers wanted a book with all the Messages, a book they could carry, a book they could have by their bed, a book they could keep in their car, a book they could give to their friends and family. I am honored and excited to fulfill this request.

I invite you to open your mind and heart to the messages that are touching so many individuals around the world during these changing times.

Blessings of grace and joy, Peggy

Morning Messages
the Eighty-eight Transmissions
from the "We Are Here" team

This is the lifetime
to honor your total
magnificent, multidimensional Self.

Message 1
It is your birthright to awaken

We have an open frequency to you. It is always, has been, will be. You decide the volume, the connection, the awareness. We have been like soft music in your background. There are times it catches your attention and times it is just there. When you vibrate joy, gratitude, love, and compassion, our contact — our presence — can stream with you into all your projects, activities, views. Fear, worry, judgments close the flow.

We invite you to make a practice of allowing yourself to still your activity and be quiet for a few minutes several times a day. As you practice and use this simple tool, it will become easier and quicker to reach your state of balance. This allows your body-mind-emotions-spirit to realign.

We encourage you and others to listen to the guidance within... to make time for stillness and be receptive to what is being offered. It is your birthright to awaken. This is the lifetime to honor your total magnificent, multidimensional Self.

You are information gatherers:
sensing, feeling, and ever expanding
from Divine Mind.

Message 2
Multidimensional Self

Humans are awakening to their multidimensional self; they are now becoming aware of how all the outside stimulation offered by your society is a way to distract and control. Pull yourselves away from some of those distractions that fill your time with activities. Allow yourselves to drop into a quiet place where you will hear our messages.

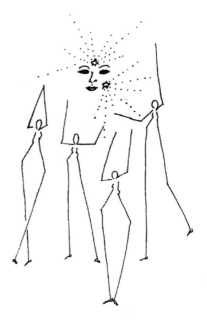

You as a human, with a body, carry within yourself a reflection of the stars, moon, and sun. You carry an aspect, a reflection, an interface with the galaxy. Remember, this is a game of evolution, a game of consciousness, a game that allows all energetic signatures to be experienced. You as human are like the most sophisticated, refined, highly developed consciousness that could be designed. You are information gatherers: sensing, feeling, and ever expanding from Divine Mind.

During these times of great change on your planet, there is a rapid-moving, strong-current river of energy. The best and most conscious manner to deal with this incredible energy... is to bravely trust the flow and allow yourself to embrace the movement and changes that are taking place. Surrender into trust, drop into a place within your being that offers you flexibility for all that is transpiring. Practice radiating joy, gratitude and appreciation into all your experiences.

... it is the pushing against
a certain reality
that adds to its strength.

MESSAGE 3
ENERGETIC PENDULUM

The energy that is bathing this planet is from the celestial realms, and beings of love and light are in partnership with those who are raising their vibrations in their personal field. Each awakened starhuman who radiates joy, gratitude, and appreciation adds a frequency, a pure vibration that joins and uplifts the entire matrix of the hologame (perceived reality).

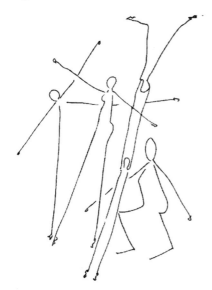

When those we hold in the darkness can be embraced by our joy, gratitude, and appreciation, there will be great shifts on the screen of reality. It is the pushing against that allows any reality to remain intact. In fact, it is the pushing against a certain reality that adds to its strength. When we are opposed to something... and express and hold a frequency of opposition... we are actually giving the very thing we oppose our energy.

The energetic pendulum will swing to either aspect of polarity. The goal is to hold one's state of mind in the perfect center of the swing — knowing that the polarities exist, knowing that there are negative and positive positions, yet recognizing that the most powerful place for your awareness is in the calm center of your being: that center and place of perfect calm... anchoring a vibration and frequency of pure joy, pure gratitude, and pure appreciation of being.

MESSAGE 4
IMAGINE YOUR EGO

Imagine your ego—like the man behind the screen in your film the "Wizard of Oz." Your ego is really just a program in the brain and this ego program thinks that it is the brain and thinks it is the self. It sends out worry and fear energy which affects the body-mind-emotions and affects your creation of reality that you then interface with.

The key to remember in ego versus Self is awareness. It is this understanding that will free the SELF. Humans are trained from infancy to believe the ego is who they are. The ego program was important as a guidance system, it was like a cruise control you have on some automobiles. It was designed to assist and be responsible for some of the function of the interface with third dimensional reality.

Another example: The desk computer has a set of programs; these programs have been created which allows you to interface with the bigger programs in the internet reality. Yet it is you who sits before the monitor and you who direct the programs. We know that you are aware that at times the programs become locked or overloaded and all that can be done is to turn off the machine.

The ego is much like these programs in the computer. They will run on automatic—yet the Self who is aware of all this can begin to make conscious adjustment to the operating systems. When one understands this they can even reprogram the entire system.

The Self can override the "worry center" or the "fear program" activated by ego.

You have the opportunity to observe how this ego program operates within your system. Notice what triggers a fear response — a worry thought. Be gentle with yourself — observe and then with great love and compassion begin to shift your energy — shift your thoughts — shift your focus. Use your "consciousness tools" and gently shift your negative non-supportive thinking. Be grateful, feel appreciation, laugh and bring joy into the moment. This is like a restart that will disengage the ego.

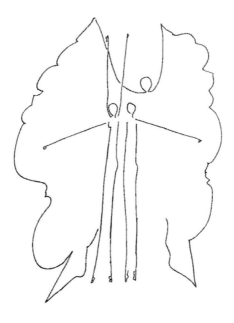

Humans are trained from infancy
to believe the ego is who they are.

... allow your consciousness to expand
and include the possibility that
there is a doorway open to other realms,
and you have a personal invitation
to walk through...

Message 5
Loving Teams

We are suggesting that you stand in the hologame — in the comfortable and familiar physical reality — and allow your consciousness to expand and include the possibility that there is a doorway open to other realms, and you have a personal invitation to walk through... There are loving teams of beings ever ready to support and guide you and all others into this new adventure. The important key to remember is the willingness and the asking. State your intentions clearly and then surrender.

Daily practices that connect you with your most Divine aspect are important...You can give yourself this gift by sitting quietly — feeling the physical body, sensing the energy

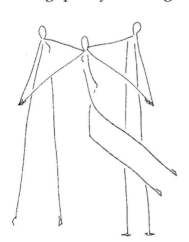

body, and, with your awareness in your heart, sending gratitude and appreciation on your breath to your Divine aspect. Allow and welcome the love and energy that flows back in return. This simple exercise will strengthen you on all levels of beingness.

Remember that energy follows thought. Watch your thoughts. Stay very vigilant with your thoughts, your emotions, and your words. Each one carries a vibration. It is your responsibility to recognize and shift the energy signature you are offering to the collective. This is far more important than you realize.

You will realize and recognize
the honor it is to be in physical embodiment—
and realize the true sacredness of all your actions.

Message 6
Dedicated Actions

It is important to understand the value of being fully, consciously present with the tasks at hand. It does not matter what you are doing or how you are doing it. The key is to be present with it, vibrating a high, pure frequency — infusing the work or the task with clear and clean vibrations of joy, gratitude, and appreciation.

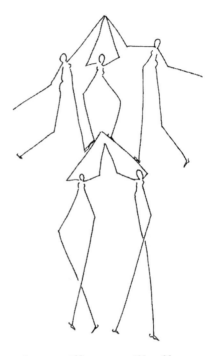

Small, simple dedicated actions — infused with joy, gratitude, and appreciation — will ripple outward from your life, shifting and transforming all other energy it touches. You and others who practice conscious stillness will offer an example, a safe harbor, and a balanced frequency for others to entrain and resonate with. Your numbers will increase.

Be gentle with yourself; lovingly bring your consciousness into each task, into each NOW, and infuse that NOW with your joy, gratitude, and appreciation. You will realize and recognize the honor it is to be in physical embodiment — and realize the true sacredness of all your actions.

Remember you are
a chalice of golden awareness.
Honor your most magnificent self
with your words and actions.

Message 7
Chalice of Golden Awareness

We invite you and the others to notice where and what you resist. Follow the thread to the source or the seed of the resistance. It is like a knot in the weaving of reality. You simply untangle it and the weaving expands.

When new awareness is offered the usual response is to resist. This resistance takes form in many ways and behaviors. Some resist outright and close their minds to the possibility of a different and more expanded reality. Some don't even see the possibility of a different and more expanded reality, their resistance is so subtle. Then there are those who see the possibility of a different and more expanded reality and they choose to make it wrong in order to hold onto the beliefs that are comfortable and their illusion of power.

Remember you are a chalice of golden awareness. Honor your most magnificent self with your words and actions. We honor you and your willingness to be an active aspect of the incredible shift of consciousness being offered into the matrix and weaving of mankind.

The best and most valuable tool you can use at this time is a vibration of joy, gratitude and appreciation. It will serve you well to practice and become proficient at calling and invoking these pure tones of resonance. It is in these frequencies that all miracles and all synchronicities unfold.

... joy, gratitude, and appreciation.
These emotions will be your life raft,
your safety in times to come.

Message 8
Your Life Raft

The physiology of the body responds to the vibrations of the emotions. When you radiate joy, happiness, gratitude, appreciation, and love, the chemicals/hormones — directives from the brain — are expansive and opening. The very cells respond to your high positive emotions.

You experience pleasant sensations throughout your entire being; your mind is clearer, your heart more open, your inner realms more expansive, and your connection to the higher realms easier and smoother.

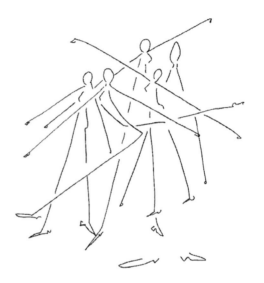

By contrast, when you experience fear, anger, or frustration, everything in the body/mind contracts. The cells and the

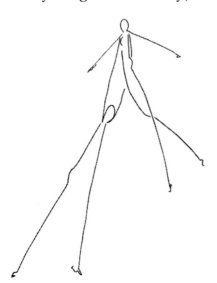

organs are bathed with stress hormones. There is a level of being closed off, with defenses up. The being is shut down; the vibrations are dense and heavy. It is important for each being to train themselves — to lift themselves up into the higher emotional vibrations, to reach for feelings of joy, gratitude, and appreciation. These emotions will be your life raft, your safety in times to come.

71

MESSAGE 9
EMOTIONS ARE A FREQUENCY

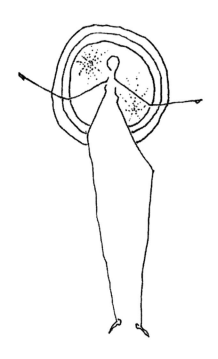

The emotional state of the human is far more important than you have been taught. Emotions are a frequency, a vibration. They interact and interface with your reality; they are your point of attraction.

They are the indicators — your sign posts, your road map... There is beauty and complexity to the unit you call your body/mind/emotions/spirit.

When the person is fearful, frightened, angry, or worried, the vibrations — the messages that the body is receiving — are very different... The functioning of the organs and muscles goes into a state of alarm. The body is on alert, separate from the whole.

When you vibrate high frequencies of joy, love, appreciation, and gratitude... all systems are in a high-vibration state of awareness: relaxed, alert, harmonious, creative. There is a flow between all atoms, all cells, and the stars.

By contrast, when you experience fear, anger, or frustration, everything in the body/mind contracts. The cells... the organs are bathed with stress hormones. There is a level of being closed off, with defenses up. The being is shut down; the vibrations are dense and heavy.

It is important for each being to train themselves—to lift themselves up into higher emotional vibrations, to reach for feelings of joy, gratitude, and appreciation. These emotions will be your life raft, your safety in times to come.

We offer this for today—when you feel an emotion or have a thought, ask yourself this question: "Is this a life-enhancing, life-giving energy, or is this thought or emotion a life-diminishing, life-harming energy?" If you practice this exercise, it will assist you in staying in a high frequency.

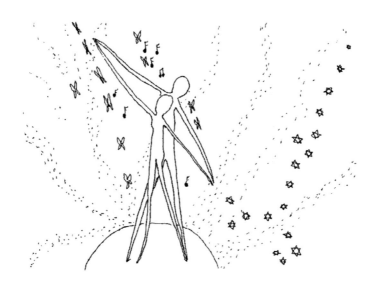

When you vibrate high frequencies
of joy, love, appreciation, and gratitude...
There is a flow between all
atoms, all cells, and the stars.

MESSAGE 10
THE SEA OF EMOTIONS

*E*ach human is a complex system of chemicals, hormones, and vibrations/frequencies as well as beliefs, programs, emotional addiction and emotional habits.

The desire to attain a balance and discover the master control, so to speak, of the emotional nature is an important aspect of each human.

Your emotions are like the sea. They ebb and flow. The sea is affected by the winds, the pull of the moon, the season. It is important for each human to realize that they can either be in the sea of emotions or riding the sea of emotions.

Awareness is the boat you build which allows you to ride the emotional waves moment to moment. It is important to realize that you are the boat and not the sea.

Remember that incomplete, unresolved, suppressed experiences that are triggered by a song, a smell, a memory will dump you into the emotional sea every time.

Get back in the boat. Remember you are not these emotions. You might feel them, yet these emotions are offering you a clear sign that you are not in your center.

In your center, in the boat of awareness, you are the master controller and navigator.

Each and everything that you personally do that reflects a vibration of joy, gratitude and appreciation enhances the matrix as a whole. These vibrations keep you in the boat above the emotional sea of turmoil and this allows you to honor your magnificence.

You can either be in the sea of emotions
or riding the sea of emotions.
Awareness is the boat you build
which allows you to ride
the emotional waves moment to moment.

You are a transformer
of energy frequencies.
You are an uplifter.

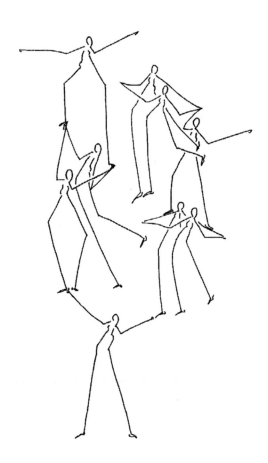

Message 11
You Are An Uplifter

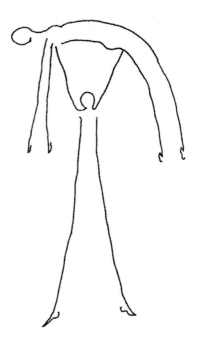

Each human comes in contact with others who resonate and carry the same frequency.

So you can look into your life experiences and see what results came from the vibrational patterns that you offered. Look into your past. We might add that you do this without judgment; just observe the experiences, the patterns, the people that you attracted, the jobs you sourced, the painful as well as the pleasant unfolding of your life experiences.

Once you have observed your life from this neutral place, you will recognize repeated patterns, habits, and repeated realities that you continue to call forth.

This knowledge is your power. Now you can begin to offer a different frequency, different feeling, and different thought. Each time you consciously make a shift to a new pattern, feeling or thought, you attract and bring forth a different result.

Remember this is a hologame, who you are, is a magnificent, powerful creator.

You are a transformer of energy frequencies. You are an uplifter.

This planet earth is heavy with dense, misqualified energy. You are here to play and bring your joy, gratitude and appreciation to this hologame. That is how the cosmic shift takes place, one heartfelt healing vibration at a time.

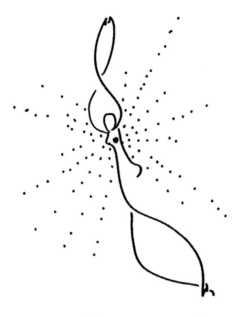

The physical unit or body was designed to support your divine presence, your soul essence, while engaged in transforming and transmuting dense low frequencies of hatred, fear, prejudice, greed, control, manipulation and self righteousness.

The physical body is a miraculous design. It was designed to continue to replicate and renew cells, tissue and bones. It was designed to be self healing. It was designed to support your spirit while your spirit accomplished its chosen mission. It was designed to support your time on this planet and your participation in this hologame.

Our goal is to assist you in the remembering that you are a multidimensional starhuman. You have a built in receptor and connection to the galaxy and all other dimensions and timeframes.

You are here to transmute energy through your heart portal, the great transformer of energy. You are a multidimensional starhuman transformer.

When you recognize your personal power, you radiate a frequency and vibration that joins other like minds to shift the global matrix.

When you hold a steady frequency of joy, gratitude and appreciation in your heart, it radiates out into the global matrix and out into the galaxy.

This frequency begins to build, it begins to increase in volume and resonance, and like a tuning fork vibrating joy, gratitude and appreciation, it activates/stimulates the same frequency resonance in others. This is service work. This is transforming work.

When you recognize your personal power,
you radiate a frequency and vibration that
joins other like minds to shift the global matrix.

When the heart is
energetically closed to others,
it is closed to the divine.
It is time that humanity
heals the wounded heart.

MESSAGE 13
SACRED HEART SPACE

It is the intelligence of the heart that offers humanity total healing and total connection with the dimensions and the stars. We have encouraged you to return to the sacred space of your heart and radiate love and appreciation to your reality. It is within the sacred heart that the alchemical process of transformation takes place.

We support and encourage you to energetically and emotionally clean out your heart space. Polish it, shine it up, air it out, and begin to live there. If the heart is energetically congested with old emotions of hurt or grief or distrust, then the richer and fuller connection with divine is distorted. When the heart is energetically closed to others, it is closed to the divine. It is time that humanity heals the wounded heart.

It is the intelligence of the heart that will guide and uplift you in all your actions. Practice asking your heart before asking your mind. Practice bridging and connecting the heart's intelligence with the brain's intelligence. Practice radiating unconditional love, joy, gratitude, and appreciation from the heart, not from the mind. Allow yourself to see your sacred heart space as spacious, infinite, expanded, and whole. It is your link to the cosmic grid. It is your way home.

Message 14
Multidimensional Transformers

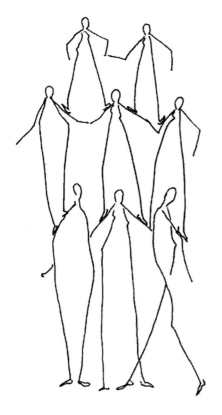

When you stay in the present moment, conscious in your own magnificence, viewing the outside events from a vibration of joy, gratitude and appreciation there is a flow.

There is a connection to the higher matrix, the divine weaving, in which all things are possible. It is through the heart portal that this higher matrix is available.

Humans are multidimensional transformers of dense low frequency vibrations.

Most humans have shut down their heart portal. They have experienced emotional pain, loss of love, betrayal and rejection. These frequencies are theirs to transform, their gifts to offer the collective.

First, each human transforms their own dense low frequency vibrations. It is their service to uplift the frequency of pain, loss of love, betrayal and rejection that is carried within their personal energy field of the heart.

Once the heart portal is cleared of any pain, real or imagined, it is now a powerful transformer and can be used in service to transform the dense frequencies of fear, hatred, prejudice and numbness that is in the collective.

There was an exercise offered by one of your sages in which you would breathe into your heart the suffering of the world and breathe it out transformed. This is a powerful alchemical practice.

Another powerful alchemical practice is offering your joy, gratitude and appreciation into each NOW.

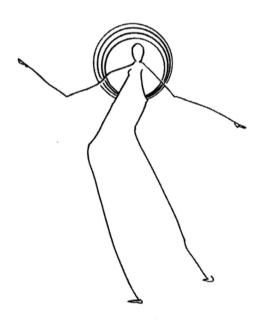

It is important for each human
to step into the magnificent ownership
of their personal multidimensional sovereignty.

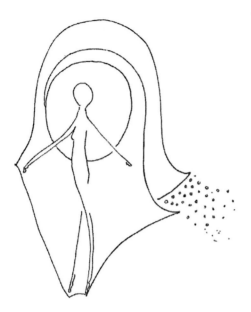

Portals exist in every form and on every level of awareness. Portals exist in all timeframes and dimensions. Portals can be subtle, obvious, hidden and secret.

A portal offers entry into another space, another state of consciousness, another reality or hologram/hologame. The fabric and weavings of your planetary energy fields are interlaced with portals.

The human body has multiple portals; the name you have given these body portals is chakra. It is through the body portals that energy and information is acquired. They open and close much like camera lenses.

These portals are the connections to the stars. They are the receptors of the frequencies from the planets, the moon and stars. They also receive data from other humans which is the unspoken. Each time two humans meet, it is their portals/chakras that share information on a deep subtle level. This happens at all times in all places with everyone.

It is the consciousness of the heart, the energy field of the heart that is the link and the connection to the divine and to life itself. The heart is the portal to the stars. The heart is the gateway to all awareness and well-being. The heart is the thinking/feeling/knowing aspect of multidimensional starhumans.

The heart is the cosmic gateway for each individual. This is the seat of your unique self. It is from the open loving conscious heart that all things unfold and all mysteries are resolved.

It is the consciousness of the heart,
the energy field of the heart that
is the link and connection
to the divine and to life itself.

Your heart is a chalice for transformation.
You are truly powerful alchemists.

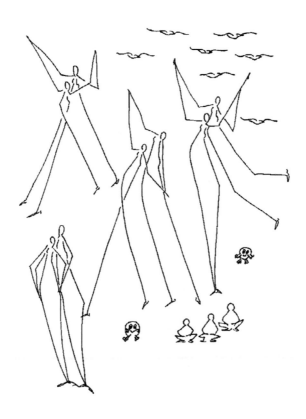

MESSAGE 16
POWERFUL ALCHEMISTS

The human body was designed to function in wholeness and balance. When this balance is disturbed by programmed beliefs, habits of thought, habits of emotional patterns, or ingesting of toxic substances in foods, there will be dis-ease within the structure of the human form. The dis-ease, or incoherent-balance, is the result of many factors over a long period of time. The imbalance will appear in areas that are vulnerable because of family patterns or beliefs from society, or a current mental toxin.

It always begins within. So look and see where you can soften and release some of the old patterns, some of the toxic emotions that you carry, the toxic beliefs in limitation that run your unconscious programs, the toxic foods that you ingest. This is the service work you are here to do — to clean up the toxins.

Now is the time to consciously... with a gentle heart... love yourself free of all limitation. We suggest that you and others continue to invite our support and assistance in your rebalancing and healing. We invite you to stay in your heart and bring anything that is not balanced, anything that is toxic, and anything that is limiting into your heart for total alchemical transformation. You are truly powerful alchemists. We know that when you decide to use this star awareness and the awesome tools available for transformation, you will shine like the most radiant star in the galaxy.

When you learn to
feel, sense, and experience joy
as the dominant vibration in your life,
you are truly free.

MESSAGE 17
COLLECT YOUR JOY

We would like you to sense and welcome joy. Let your self examine the feeling of joy. When are you filled with joy? What are the conditions? What is the situation?

We invite you to practice the awareness of joy—being in the vibration, the feeling, the emotion of joy. Your body chemistry will change when you bring an awareness of joy into your moments.

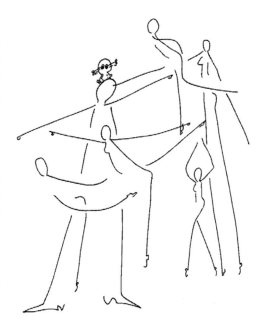

Over time, you will understand that joy is a natural state of being. It is a Vibrational way out of the mass consciousness grid. It is the ladder, the rope, the lifejacket. When you learn to feel, sense, experience joy as the dominant vibration in your life, you are free. When you hold a joy vibration more often than any other emotion, you are in a position of powerful creating. You are in the Divine flow.

We urge you to journey back in time and recall when you were taught to not express your joy... When did you shut down the avenues to your joy? When the events were emotionally painful, you closed down the vibrations of joy/appreciation/gratitude/love and carried the denser vibrations of fear, rejection, and anger. Go back... and bring into memory one of the higher-frequency emotions. Go back and collect your joy, like a game of finding the golden egg.

MESSAGE 18
MAGIC CARPET

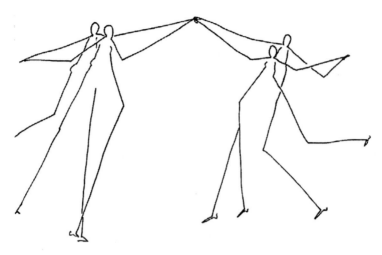

When you maintain a pure high joyful expression of gratitude, it is your magic carpet as well as your protective shield... to ride the winds of change and the vibrational frequencies of any timeframe or reality. So as often as you possibly can, return to your sacred heart and allow the divine love of the universe to radiate out to all. You are a carrier of this divine love, as are all humans. The key is to remember this power and this purpose while in a physical body and to maintain an open heart for this divine love to flow through.

The well-being and care of this sacred heart space is most important, and the vibrational frequency is the resonance of joy and gratitude. This is a message that we continue to restate often, because it is the only true message. You—and everyone—are purely a vibrational being. Practice raising your vibrations at all times.

Sing, dance, love, forgive, honor, acknowledge, praise, and appreciate with a grateful heart all that is before you, all that you experience, all that you see or feel. These emotional vibrations and frequencies are your magic wand to transform all other discordant frequencies and vibrations.

A pure high joyful
expression of gratitude
is your magic carpet.

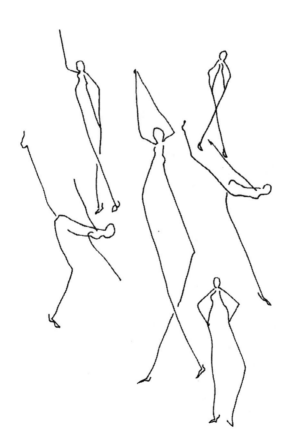

MESSAGE 19
JOY IS AN ELIXIR

Joy is a high vibration; joy moves your energy smoothly and effortlessly throughout your body. Gratitude is a high vibration. It is an elixir; it uplifts the vibration. All aspects of the body-mind relax when you are in a state of gratitude. Appreciation is a high vibration... When you allow a sincere feeling of appreciation to radiate from your heart, you are working with transformational energy. Love is a high vibration... Love is your Divine essence.

Visualize a past experience that is contaminated with your guilt or regret, and in your mind's eye create a new result. Imagine you acting or saying something different, something more loving or more conscious. Allow yourself to feel or sense a different emotion—one of joy, gratitude, or appreciation. Continue to use this visualization exercise until the past experience has lost its charge.

Each individual is responsible for the emotions they offer to the collective. The question to ask is, "Are the emotions I am experiencing right now adding to the accumulation of fear, anger, and powerlessness, or are they contributing to the uplifting of consciousness—my personal consciousness as well as the collective?" If they are not uplifting consciousness... do all that is within your power to shift your feelings.

Each individual is responsible
for the emotions they offer
to the collective.

Each time you transform
an old pattern of fear or struggle,
you are doing global service work
at a personal level.

MESSAGE 20
GLOBAL SERVICE WORK

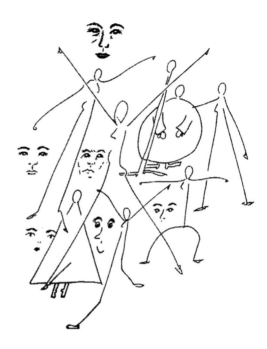

*E*motions are designed to act as guidelines to show you when you are off course. When you are feeling fear, it is valuable to express that in the moment, "I am feeling some fear right now." You don't have to know where the feelings are coming from, or what they mean; you just have to acknowledge them. Once they are acknowledged, they are defused. They are not stored in your system.

Each time you personally transform an old pattern of fear or struggle, you are uplifting an energetic piece of the dysfunctional matrix. You are uplifting your personal vibration. Each time you shift an emotional response from anger or judgment to love, joy, gratitude, and acceptance, you are doing global service work at a personal level. Each time you come together with other awake, multidimensional beings, you are strengthening the power of your global service work.

The gift you can offer to the collective by your embodiment is the gift of a pure, high vibrational frequency. A pure high vibrational frequency is held in joy, gratitude, and appreciation. Remember to maintain this frequency, or return to it as often and quickly as possible. Each moment is an opportunity to shift the long-held dysfunctional vibrations of lack, fear, anger, judgment, and unworthiness.

MESSAGE 21
STARSELF TO SHINE

As humans awake from their unconscious slumber, that numb place in consciousness where denial is the frequency and the guest—as the cosmic energy continues to increase and floods the consciousness of mankind with the spark of their own knowing and power—more and more angry people will rise out of their numb slumber and begin to protest the dysfunctional conditions in which they are living. You can see or sense the unrest, the protests, and the anger that are manifesting around the globe.

Your service work... and the service work of all multidimensional starhumans who are awake and aware... is to hold a steady pure frequency of love, joy, gratitude, and appreciation. This frequency and this resonance of these pure, high vibrations will act as the foundation and the anchoring that allows for the new paradigm, as everything is shifting and moving into the higher dimensions.

You, along with others, have your own personal denseness to uplift and transform, as well as holding the frequency of the high vibrations for others to resonate with. Allow yourself to laugh, play, be in your joy, be in your heart, and be in your full appreciation of this wonderful game. Remember you are as big as the stars. 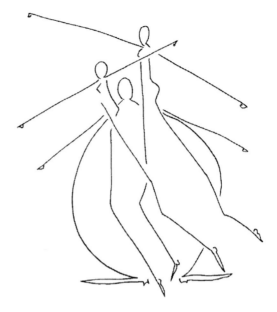 This body and this life are only a small reflection of your magnificence. Allow and invite the fullness of your starself to shine into your life.

Your service work
—as a multidimensional starhuman—
is to hold a steady, pure frequency
of love, joy, gratitude, and appreciation.

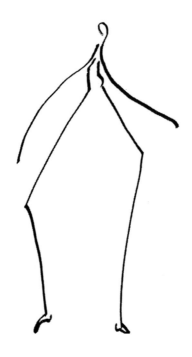

Life is always an inside job.
You are always the key...
you are the creator,
you are the observer,
you are the lover,
and you are the loved.

MESSAGE 22
LIFE IS AN INSIDE JOB

*E*motional spins, as you call them, are usually the results of your reality not meeting your expectations. There is usually an old mental program running. When this happens, you are looking outside yourself for validation, as well as satisfaction. The picture of what you want in your life and the actual reality of your life are not a match. Remember this is an illusion. Everything is created within and then projected out. So the key is to look within and see the unfulfilled expectation within.

Life is always an inside job. You are always the key... you are the creator, you are the observer, you are the lover, and you are the loved. So be gentle with yourself and return to that space within where you honor your joy and gratitude. Those are the vibrations, the stepping stones out of the emotional spins.

At this time, it is easy to drop into the mass consciousness grid. There is much chaos and distress happening everywhere, and it can be a fragile emotional path to walk with all the images and the awareness of the death, destruction, loss, and anguish happening in the collective grid. The responsibility of you and other multidimensional starhumans is to anchor a strong vibration of love, joy, gratitude, and appreciation. Any other emotion only adds to the collective anguish.

MESSAGE 23
A TIMELESS PORTAL

Imagine the skill needed to walk a tightrope; each step is in the now. If walkers allow themselves to think about the steps beyond the current one, they lose their focus and they lose their balance. It is by staying in the now, all energy focused on the current step, the task in the moment, that they complete the walk successfully.

When you stay present in each moment you are more available and able to hear clear guidance. Artists who begin to paint and become so focused that they lose all track of time are creating in each new now. When you remain focused in each new now, there is a flow of creating that unfolds with grace and ease.

You are always creating. So you are either creating from the past or you are creating from the now. If you are creating from the past, all your creation will be flavored with your past memories, past feelings, past regrets, past beliefs.

However when you learn to create in the fresh now, it is like a new canvas. If you stay in the past you create from the past; if you project your awareness into the future, you are also creating from the past.

Once this skill is mastered in your personal activities and hologame, you will become aware that each present NOW is a portal. A timeless portal.

When you remain focused

in each new now,

there is a flow of creating that

unfolds with grace and ease.

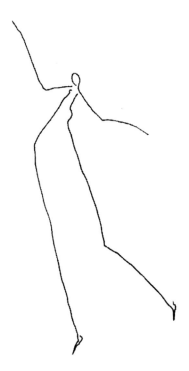

MESSAGE 24
ENERGETIC STANCE

There is a mental state of mind and an emotional state of being that we invite you to maintain. When you bring your awareness into the present moment of NOW and you are holding an energetic stance of a high vibration, it does not matter what you are doing or with whom you are doing it.

The key is to be in the moment, fully filled with your joy, gratitude and appreciation. There will be a flow, a grace and an ease. It is not what you do, but how you do each moment.

The illusions of struggle, stress and strain are low frequencies, and these states of mind vibrate/radiate in the third dimension. They are a part of the matrix of lock-down.

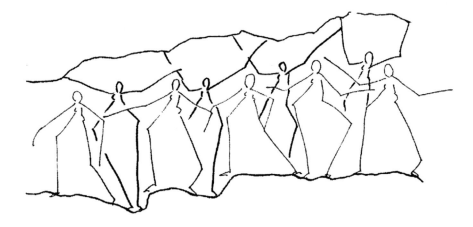

Become aware that you hold the illusion of struggle, difficulty, and challenges; these are states of mind that are learned as part of the third dimension. They are part of the collective limitations of lack and powerlessness.

There is an awareness occurring in the consciousness of humans—that they are unlimited; they are only playing a hologame that appears to have limitation. This is an illusion.

These illusions of limitation are passed down from parent to child; they are only beliefs. These limitations are encouraged and maintained by your society; they are supported by the media, and by your leaders. Limitation is the old third dimensional paradigm.

There is an evolution of consciousness happening in the hearts and minds of more and more humans who are waking up to the realization that they are the creators of their experience.

This evolution of consciousness expands into the truth of the unlimited self—into the awareness, and the aspect of each human becoming conscious of their lives in multiple realities.

It is not what you do,
but how you do each moment.

The highest and grandest service
you can offer others is your
full divine presence in the NOW.

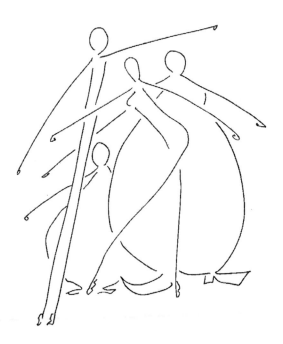

MESSAGE 25
ILLUSIONS OF LIMITATIONS

There is magic, there is alchemical power available to each starhuman who learns to ride the wave of energy that is creating all the NOW's. It is a skill, it is a game. Practice today as you go about your mundane tasks to anchor divine energy into the moment. Practice returning to your full awareness. Practice stepping out of your habitual thoughts that run your unconscious activities. Practice being fully present in the present moment.

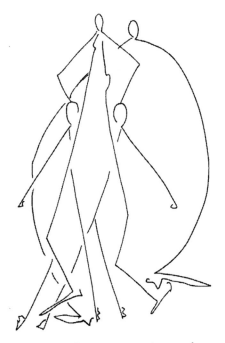

The place to start is the heart center. When you place your awareness in your heart you will naturally dwell in the NOW. It is the mind that likes to play in the realms of past and future. It is the mind that dwells in the game of "what if" and "if only"... the game of regrets and sorrows. It is the mind that entertains fear and hatred. It is the programs of the mind that keep each multidimensional starhuman locked in the illusion of limitations.

This is the highest and grandest service you can offer others: your full divine presence, your full divine presence in the NOW. Bring your full consciousness to each moment and you will be embraced by your joy and gratitude. This joy and gratitude will bubble up from your sacred heart and radiate out to all. Then every activity, every encounter will be uplifted into the realms of light and love. You will begin to live in the sacred alchemical portal of the NOW.

Message 26
Global Shift

Humans are awakening to realize that they are not limited by their physical body. They are not limited by their beliefs of time. They are not limited. Humanity is awakening to its magnificent multidimensional expression of Divine Mind.

This dimension, this reality has had a lock-down. Your skills and abilities were being honed just to be in a physical body. There were spans of time when that experience of being physical was your focus, and the other aspects receded into the background. Now your codes are activated; you are beginning to step into your role in the divine unfoldment of the next evolution of consciousness.

The world is experiencing a global shift... More people are moving from the grid of fear, separation, and manipulation into the conscious, aware state of mind and experience—of truly owning their personal power and their personal actions as a part of the Divine whole. They are awakening... to the knowing that they are multidimensional, to acceptance of their role in the global and galactic transformation. This is accomplished by awareness of their personal power—awareness of how their actions/thoughts/words affect the whole.

Humans are awakening...
to the knowing that they are multidimensional,
and to the acceptance of their role
in the global and galactic transformation.

We offer you the gentle reminder
to be easy with yourself
and be easy with others.

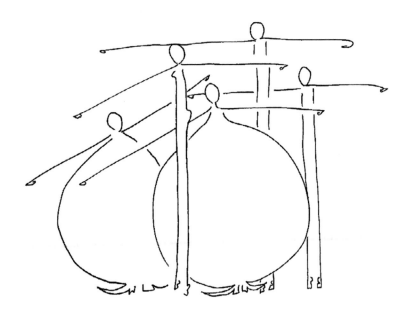

MESSAGE 27
TEACHING ENVIRONMENT

The human being is offered a multitude of possible realities in each moment, and with each decision... Give yourself the opportunity to realize that with every decision, you had the choice of a myriad of outcomes, each reality worthy of the experience. It is only your limited thinking that tells you one is better than the other.

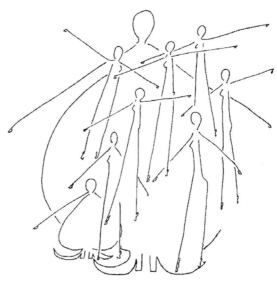

You are beings of great contrast. This planet is a "teaching environment" of opposites. Your goal is to see the contrast and hold them both without judging or becoming polarized. It is the judging that keeps this type of energy intact — this "warring within" and "warring without." Judging holds you in its tight grip of conflict. There is no peace in the mind that judges. Peace comes when you learn to hold/ allow the contrast in the transforming alchemical energy of your heart awareness.

We offer you, as a tool, the gentle reminder to be easy with yourself, be easy with others. When you notice you are in a stance or mindset of judging, gently allow your consciousness to float above the contrast of the polarities, until you can see that they are only opposite sides of the same hand. See that they are a part of the same program unfolding. Go to your heart; hold the conflict — the contrast — there, until the energy of the heart transforms the contrast.

MESSAGE 28
UNIVERSAL MATRIX

We observe the busyness that humans are so skilled with. We actually marvel at the various and diverse ways that most humans use their time, energy, and focus. This is the physical reality, and the goal here is to understand, manage, and transform energy that is dense and limiting—to bring consciousness to everything.

So the highest truth, in actuality, is that any activity that the human performs offers the incredible opportunity to infuse that activity with the purest consciousness and presence. The key to that statement is "purest consciousness and presence."

It is the habit of most humans to stay in their minds and the activities of their thoughts.

They give these thoughts much of their power, they allow the mind to be in control of the energy that is moving through the body. While in their thoughts and in their mind, they respond automatically; much like a robot, they complete one task and move to the next task totally disconnected from their heart center, their feelings and their power.

It is time to develop the keen awareness that no matter what you are doing in your daily life, it is affecting the entire universal matrix. We repeat: Anything you are doing.

An example is the job of taking out the trash; this mundane activity can be a moment of divine transformation for you and for the energy grid if you bring your full divine presence into the moment and the activity. You can infuse the trash with the light in such a manner that wherever it goes it also shifts the surrounding energy of everything and everyone it touches.

It is time to develop the keen awareness
that no matter what you are doing
in your daily life, it is affecting
the entire universal matrix.

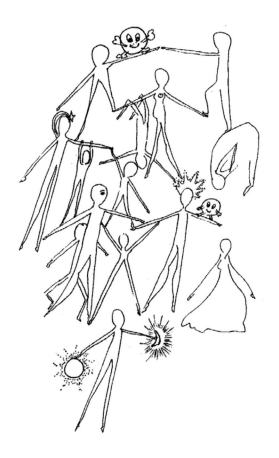

You are multidimensional
in nature and function.

MESSAGE 29
EACH DIMENSION IS AVAILABLE

Being in human form is only one aspect of who you are. As a physical being focused on... this third dimension, it seems to you as if that is all that is. It feels real, looks real; yet it is only one perspective of the multidimensional aspects of what a human/being actually is. Each dimension is available to you at all times. Each is resonating at a different frequency. As more and more beings become conscious, these other realities/dimensions will begin to appear.

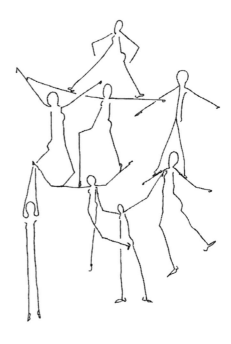

Your sages and wise ones have all spoken of the ability to shift from... one state of awareness to another. They have offered suggestions of prayer, meditation, fasting. Shamans and mystics have offered mind-altering herbs and ceremonies of dance and drums to bring a shift of consciousness... All these suggestions and techniques are for the important purpose of shifting your awareness — to understand that the world you view is only one small perspective of the whole.

Remember, you are a consciousness and an aspect of Divine Mind. You are multidimensional in nature and function. How the multidimensional aspect of yourself manifests depends on your belief systems, your expanded awareness, and your openness to all possibilities.

Imagine the human is like a radio—
able to move the dial from one station
or spectrum of consciousness
to another with ease.

MESSAGE 30
MYRIAD REALITIES

As a multidimensional being, you are at all times operating on many levels and dimensions... We are here to encourage you and others to recognize and honor the myriad realities in which you have a presence at all times. The day-to-day aspect of a human being's life is only one small fraction of what is taking place in the matrix that they hold.

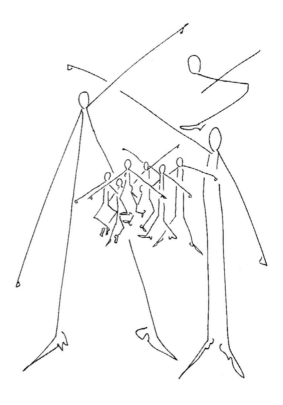

Imagine the human is like your radio; each station or frequency invites one type of music. Most people never move the dial to explore the other signals, the other connections.

The focus is limited to what that one frequency provides, what information that one frequency offers. A person who is aware of their multidimensional self is able to move the dial from one station to the other with ease. They allow for more stimulation, more information, and a broader spectrum of consciousness.

Again, we invite you to expand your awareness to include more of your multidimensional beingness. It is much easier than one might imagine. You do it often. Now, just recognize when you have shifted.

Message 31
Play With Time

Time is one of the fabrics of your earthly game. It is a veil; it keeps you in the illusion. It is wise to realize that time is created only to serve a certain aspect of physical reality.

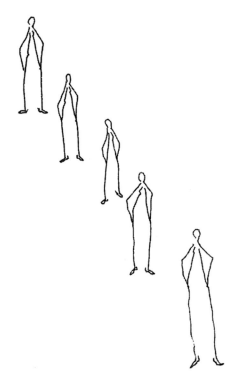

Imagine a large moving walkway like you have in your airports; the moving walkway is time. You step into the belief of time, and it moves you, or you move with it. Now expand your vision to see the entire airport, expand to the entire parking area, expand to the planes arriving and taking off. The moving walkway is only a small aspect of the entire airport. Time, like the moving walkway, is really a very small aspect of the entire universe.

We invite you to play with time... stretch it... mold it. See if you can grab some. Step out of time... step into time. Be aware of your beliefs of time and continue to expand beyond them. Be gentle with yourself. Remember the importance of laughter. Practice laughing at time. Take time to laugh. Fill your time with laughter.

We invite you to play with time...
stretch it... mold it.
See if you can grab some.
Step out of time... step into time.

Your reality is blinking on and off at all times. The human brain connects the individual frames into one continuous movement.

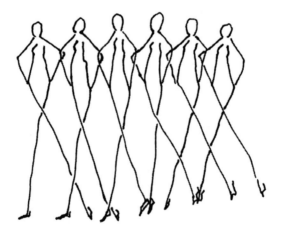

MESSAGE 32
BLINKING ON AND OFF

Your reality is blinking on and off at all times. The human brain was designed to sense the "on" frequency. Just as quickly, it blinks "off," and all disappears. However, your brain registers and connects only the "on" segments, and thus you have the sense or feeling of your reality being solid. It is an illusion. It is the hologame creation.

An example of this is your movies, which are not one continuous movement that you view with your eyes. Instead, they are frames of action strung together and projected one after the other at a quick speed. The human brain connects the individual frames into one continuous movement.

The "off" position is the space in which all creation is formed. Your highest soul self dwells in this place. It is from this place that seeming miracles are created, that synchronicities unfold, and that the wonder and magic of physical reality is formed. It is a place we invite you to begin to consciously travel. This is done by shifting your perception, shifting your focus from the seeming solidness of your daily life to the expanse of all that is holding your reality in place. This shift can be created by quieting the outer mind in mediation... the exercise of following your breath to the door of the stillness.

MESSAGE 33
MOLD AND SCULPT ENERGY

It is an illusion that things stay the same. Your reality is always in flux. Each moment is offered new and ready for the imprint. The conscious or even the unconscious old habits, rigid beliefs which tell the fresh new energy what it is that you expect in your given reality. Each person is actively in each moment creating the reality or the illusion of their reality in which they live and believe they exist.

The idea that you recreate your environment moment-to-moment is a bit overwhelming and certainly a challenge to a mindset which finds comfort in sameness. Ideas of this nature, causes an inner conflict between what you think you know about your reality and what is the cosmic truth about your reality.

Quantum Physics is offering insights into multi-dimensional realities. Quantum Physics is showing that energy can be a particle or a wave. Energy is imprinted by your conscious or unconscious thoughts. Each moment is fresh, awaiting your command so to speak.

There are those awakening to the realization that they are more than who they thought themselves to be. They are truly multi-dimensional beings, aware that reality is a thought, reality is a particle, and reality is a wave. These beings are beginning to ride the energy in a new way. They are beginning to mold and sculpt energy with more loving consciousness.

Your reality is always in flux.
Each moment is offered new
and ready for the imprint.

Ride your breath.
Dwell in your sacred heart space
no matter what is happening around you.

MESSAGE 34
RIDE YOUR BREATH

It is important for you and other humans who are sensitive to the subtle energy signature of others, as well as the personal interaction with other matrixes, to take the time to keep your own personal energy field clear, clean, and centered.

There is a higher level of stress and discordant energy happening on all fronts. Remember to stay in your pure calm center and radiate the vibration of joy, gratitude, and appreciation. These vibrations will reflect and deflect any discordant or disturbing energy fields that you encounter. The more conscious and responsible each starhuman becomes in creating a coherent energy field within and then radiating it out to all, the greater the service to mankind.

Ride your breath. Dwell in your sacred heart space. No matter what is happening around you, no matter what energy matrix you encounter, continue to anchor and hold a pure high vibration in the midst of any discordant fearful emotions and energy signature. Ask for support from the realms of truth and light. There are beings of divine love who can and will embrace you in an energy matrix of upliftment and protection.

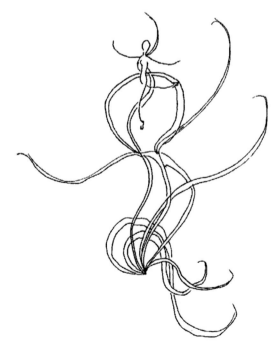

As you send your energy forth,
several realities are always possible.
The reality that manifests is the one on which
you have focused more of your energy.

MESSAGE 35
PARALLEL REALITIES

Everything you experience as solid and "real" is a vibration of energy — held, or locked in place, by belief systems. If, for a moment, you could set aside all mental programs about your reality, you would experience an entirely different perspective of what you call reality.

We would like you to receive the idea that there are several realities, several outcomes, several parallel realities that could always manifest... You and others are broadcasting energy in the form of your thoughts, your emotions, and your beliefs at all times. As you send the energy forth, several realities are always possible. The reality that manifests is the one on which you have focused more of your energy.

You have a television in your home. Even though it is turned off at this time, you could simply activate it and there would be a program or news or movie... Your brain is much like the TV; you can switch the channels. You can find a memory of the past that invokes emotions, or you can review a channel of your worries, or you can envision and get a sense of your possible futures. We are encouraging you to... embrace the countless realities that are only a frequency, a vibration away.

Message 36
Blueprint or Template

All life forms on planet earth are held as a blueprint or template in the subtle realms. This energy grid, this matrix, the sacred geometry of the universe, the master pattern is held in the sixth dimension.

Each human being resides focused on planet earth in the third and four dimensions, however as a multidimensional being there are aspects of each human that also resides in the other dimensions. It is from the sixth dimension that the template of who you are in your present form is held. It is the sixth dimension which holds these master patterns.

The matrices of your reality are made up of the individual matrixes or energy grids coming together in a new form or weavings. Remember everything that exists here in form has a matrix. It is these energy fields, these matrices that form larger energy fields and hold the collective thought forms and beliefs of mass consciousness.

What you see and sense as solid and in physical form is only this matrix. It is from this matrix that all change within the human form can be made. The concept that everything is first energy vibrations before it is form has been taught by your sages and wise awake ones.

This is a message which reminds humans that they are more than just the body. They are a part of the divine unfoldment. They are multidimensional, existing on many levels and dimensions at the same time.

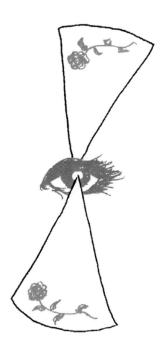

The concept that everything is
first energy vibrations before it is form
has been taught by your sages
and wise awake ones.

The universe is a complex matrix.
It is a weaving of energy
strands of all possibilities.

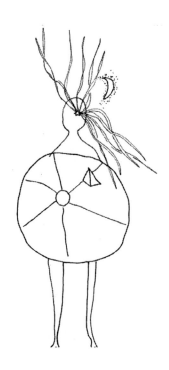

MESSAGE 37
CREATORS OF YOUR HOLOGAME

The truth is that the other dimensions are as close as your breath and allowing. This knowledge scares most humans. It does not fit with the learned programs. It is too strange.

The idea that the stars communicate with every cell of your physical body at all times can be a mental stretch for some. The concept that someone can hear this communication from the stars and act upon the connection is a real mental stretch.

The universe is a complex matrix. It is a weaving of energy strands of all possibilities. It is waves and it is particles depending upon the focus and the awareness of the focuser. Remember you are the creators of your hologame.

Reality, as most humans believe and sense it to be, is limited to what they can see, feel and touch. However there is a much larger universe that is available in which parallel realities exist and portals of energy can be activated or closed or shielded. Traveling dimensions is merely a shifting of one's consciousness, frequency, or vibration.

We invite you to continue to listen to spirit and the stars. We honor those who are willing to expand their sense of who they are and to recognize and allow their multidimensional aspects to be acknowledged.

Portals, matrices, energy grids, power places, star travel, parallel lives and realities, dimensional shifts—these are all juicy places to focus on and invite into your daily life.

*E*arth is a sea of vibrations and frequencies. Mankind is skilled in creating and inventing devices in which there is an energy frequency and vibration. These waves of energy are always moving through you.

All the electrical devices in your home — every light, the phone systems, computers, the kitchen appliances all give off a frequency. The television is one of the major contributors of discordant frequencies. Most people are not aware of these frequencies. They have tuned them out; their energy field has adjusted and learned to live with them.

This planet is woven with electronic frequencies. If you had the vision to see the strands of energy connecting all the power lines, electrical devices, cell phones, televisions and microwaves you would be amazed at how tightly woven this energetic matrix truly is. It surrounds your planet in an energetic grid of discordant frequencies.

These electronic frequencies are always affecting the physical body, the mental state of mind. They are a part of the hypnotizing that takes place in this hologame. These electronic frequencies are addictive to your energy field; they hold a certain mindset in place. Be aware of these discordant frequencies and the matrix that they create. You will be less affected by discordant frequencies when you stay anchored and firm in your own personal energy field.

The solar flares, the galactic bursts of energy are surging through this shield of hypnotizing electronic frequencies, activating certain aspects of the DNA codes. These cosmic energy thrusts are a wake up call to humanity. The earth's magnetic field holds the higher integrity of the hologame in place. This is being overridden by the electronic fields.

We invite you to continue to maintain a strong energy field of love, joy and appreciation. When you vibrate these high coherent frequencies, you will not be affected by the bombardment of the planetary electronic grid. You create a cohesive field.

We invite you to maintain
a strong energy field of
love, joy and appreciation,
to create a cohesive field.

You can begin to untangle
any aspect of your personal matrix
by the very thoughts that
you hold and express.

Message 39
Personal Matrix

We want to share the importance of recognizing and honoring your own personal matrix, your vibrational field and how it is holding and forming your daily reality.

It is from this personal matrix that the life you experience and the body expression that you experience is created.

The personal matrix is affected by all that it encounters. From the moment of conception, all the while the body is being formed in the mother's womb, there is an exchange and blending of the matrix. The family genetics are woven into the matrix; your parents' strongly held beliefs and emotions are woven into your personal matrix. The years of childhood, the experiences and encounters are woven into the personal matrix. The experiences that are painful, scary, fearful, limiting in any way are also woven in, as a blockage or tangle of your energy flow.

It is these blockages and tangles that we would like to assist each human in releasing so there is a flow once again from your divine blueprint.

Remember energy follows thought. You can begin to untangle any aspect of your personal matrix by the very thoughts that you hold and express.

Vibrational medicine works on these subtle levels to untangle and release any blockages held from past memory or even the tangles that were given at birth from the family matrix. This work that is being done by awakened beings; it is coming in many forms and ways.

Just imagine that there could be
several aspects of you existing here
in the dimension of planet earth
at the same time.

Message 40
Time Is Fluid

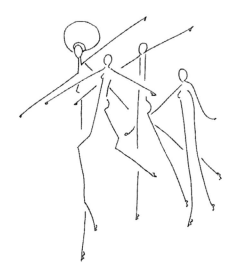

What if time is fluid? How would that affect your day and the participation in your earthly life? Just for a moment, let us imagine that past, present, and future are all happening and shifting simultaneously. It is only your perception that places them in the rigid placement. Imagine that events in your future could shift the events from your past, which would alter your present NOW. As a multidimensional being, this is how you would and could address this concept called time.

As a human, you are engaged with time because it is one of the matrices of this planetary game. However, as a multidimensional being, you can and do step out of this earthly limited matrix of time. It is a matter of awareness and a matter of practice.

Let us plant this seed: just imagine that there could be, might be, several aspects of you existing here in the dimension of planet earth at the same time — each aspect of you living entirely different lives in different cultures, different everything. As multidimensional beings, it is actually very simple to have more than one game piece in the game at the same time. This is just an energetic stretch for your awareness. In the meantime, be in your joy; notice your thoughts; and continue to honor all your experiences, from your current perspective. The rest will follow in an easy manner.

Humans are beginning to shift
their beliefs of what is real,
and as they do,
their reality begins to shift.

MESSAGE 41
REALITY IS MUCH LIKE WATER

Reality is much like water. It can change and morph into many different forms depending on the conditions and energy. It can be solid, hard as ice. It can be fluid and flowing as liquid, and it can be buoyant and light like steam. Most humans prefer to relate to their reality in its frozen state. However reality has the capabilities of shifting into several different aspects. It is still reality just as water is still water whether it is frozen, liquid, or steam.

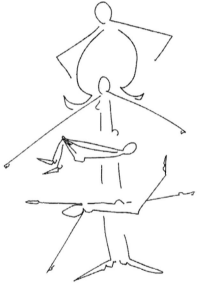

That is just an example of how your third dimension can and does respond to your beliefs and projection, your energy signature, and your understanding of what you perceive as real and how that is manifested on the screen of this hologame.

Humans are beginning to shift their beliefs of what is real, and as they do, their reality begins to shift. They notice the shift and continue to expand their awareness to include these new perceptions. You and others are becoming conscious and aware that you are multidimensional humans. It is like stairs; with each step you have a larger vista to observe.

The future and the past exist
only because that belief
was installed upon your entry.

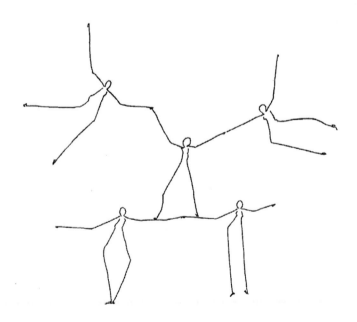

Message 42
Explore the Possibilities

In the dream state, all realities are accepted as real. It is in the dream state that humans experience their multidimensional self as well as their parallel selves.

Just for the moment allow yourself to consider that, since all time is simultaneous, there are parallel lives going on in tandem. The future and the past exist only because — in the three-dimensional reality on planet earth — that belief was installed upon your entry.

There are numerous other lives in which you as the wondrous celestial multidimensional starbeing are fully active and living in another timeframe and perhaps even in another dimension. These other aspects of self that are living entirely different realities and lifetimes are as active and focused in the reality in which they are living as you are in the reality in which you are living.

Most humans have such a difficult time handling the one reality — the one life they are focused on — that the idea of having more than one life going on at the same time is very overwhelming and difficult to comprehend. We say to those who feel a bit overwhelmed to gently allow themselves to explore the possibilities in a playful, lighthearted manner.

It is valuable to meditate, walk,
and allow quietness and creativity to flow.
It is in these places that you
gently slip into another dimension.

Message 43
Straddling Multi-Realities

There is always an ebb and flow between the states of consciousness. This is something that everyone is dealing with right now on your planet, the bridging of two or more different levels of consciousness or the straddling of multi-realities.

You are free to travel the other realities and dimensions. It is just a matter of where you place your attention. Remember energy follows thought. So shift your thoughts and shift your feeling nature, and you will throw off your limited beliefs, and the limited net that would keep you anchored to only one reality.

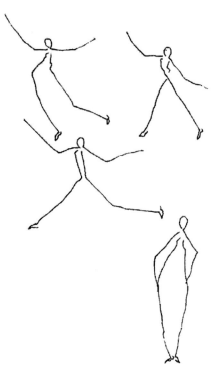

The important thing to remember is that constant interaction with others can be a distraction to the subtle ability to alter your awareness and shift your focus to the nested dimensions in which you dwell. That is why it is valuable to meditate, walk, and allow quietness and creativity to flow. It is in these places that you gently slip into another dimension. The goal that is being offered is the awareness that you are not alone and that you can easily connect with the non-physical support systems.

However, what is required of you, and anyone who seeks this connection, is to make space for it to happen.

MESSAGE 44
RIDE THE WIND STREAM

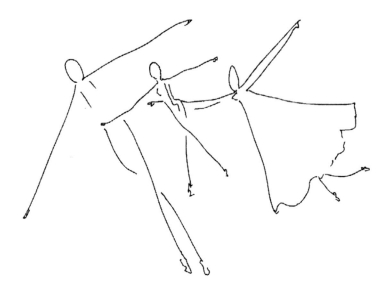

You can observe your hawks that soar above the meadow. They move into the flow of the wind stream and are carried aloft with only a slight feather movement.

It is the human ego that has been programmed to struggle, to stray off course, to lose focus, intent and passion.

The ultimate aim of endeavor for the awakened starhuman is the knowledge that there is a divine flow or wind stream in which all things expand with ease and grace. You even have a term for this demonstration; it is called a miracle. A miracle is considered supernatural, a phenomenon, and a rarity.

When the hawk soars effortlessly on the wind stream, he does not consider it a miracle; he considers it wisdom. He knows he is one with the flow of energy and he rides it.

The wind stream is created by the vibrations that are being offered to the matrix. When individuals are holding a frequency of joy, gratitude and appreciation, they move through their lives effortlessly — like the hawk soaring.

The consciousness of the universe delights in bringing results in wondrous ways. In that space, your clear intention is manifest in the quickest and easiest way possible.

If you are struggling or efforting with anything, stop and reset the vibrations you are sending to the field — if you are struggling or efforting with anything. Be a conscious monitor of your thoughts, feelings and projections.

The consciousness of the universe
delights in bringing results
in wondrous ways.

MESSAGE 45
SWIFT FLOWING ENERGY

During these times of great change on your planet, imagine there is a strong rapid moving river of energy. This dynamic and powerful energy current that is washing over your planet is moving through all aspects of life, bathing every cell and atom of the body with a frequency of transformation and evolution.

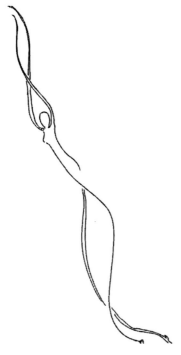

When you surrender to this rapid flowing current of transformation you move with it, you become a part of it, like a small twig that floats upon the surface of the water.

Yet if you cling to the shores of old patterns, old familiar emotions, old dysfunctional behaviors, you will be battered and will tire. If you fight the energy current or doubt its power, you will be overwhelmed.

The best and most conscious manner to deal with this incredible energy that is gifted to humanity is to bravely trust the flow and embrace the movement and changes that are taking place. Surrender into trust. Drop into a place within your being that offers you flexibility of all that is transpiring. Surrender to the flow.

There are millions who are awakening and understanding the divine manifestation. As a guardian of light you are most powerful and effective when you maintain a high frequency vibration.

You are more fully connected with divine source and guided to the places and people that are ready and willing to shift. You will offer a vibration which will trigger awareness in others, a vibration which will anchor a new expanded consciousness. You will offer a life raft to those who are willing to trust their divine natures and surrender to the essence that they are magnificent beings of divine light.

The best and most conscious manner
to deal with this incredible energy
that is gifted to humanity
is to bravely trust the flow
and embrace the movement and
changes that are taking place.

MESSAGE 46
PLAYING THE HOLOGAME

The third dimension is time and space, where the physical and the non-physical intersect. So imagine you are a being of Light consciousness and you decide to enter this third dimension, this game board, this hologame, this life, which has certain rules and requirements. The first rule is you must enter the game under the veil of forgetfulness, you must enter unaware that you are a divine being of Light.

Before you step into the game of third dimension you plan your strategy. You set your goals and your trials; you select the talents, strengths and abilities you will develop. These will not be totally veiled. You select which aspect of the game board of life you will participate in, the family group you will be a part of. You preset the conditions from your highest awareness and highest consciousness. All of these arrangements and conditions are taking place in non-physical pure consciousness.

Once all this has been preset, your goals and the desired experiences that you would like to collect, there is an excitement to be joining this third dimensional hologame on planet earth called life. To enter this dimension, you acquire a game piece called a physical body, which is much like a computer. You must honor the rules of the game in order to play in physical form. The game board is set in space and time and your awareness is veiled in forgetfulness.

In the beginning of the game, you believe you are the physical body. The final condition of the game is a wild card, so to speak, that no matter how well you planned or how well you preset your conditions of the game while you were in your non-physical form, this part of the game is only revealed once you have committed and taken on the physical body. These conditions, these aspects, are an unknown. They are your challenges. It is these aspects that offer the most opportunity, the most growth.

The challenges could be in the beginning, the middle, or end of your personal game. They will appear as the most difficult aspect of being in a physical body. They might be a mental, emotional, or physical challenge, or a combination of all three. They will offer you the quickest way to your preset goals.

The goal of this game is to be able to totally remove the veil of forgetfulness to your awareness of your most divine Light, magnificent Self and to laugh and celebrate knowing who you truly are.

Today we invite you to play full out.
Enjoy all the wondrous gifts
that this life game offers.

Message 47
Personal Sovereignty

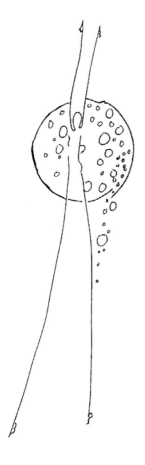

The key to experiencing the magic and miracles in your life is the level of allowing and the focused clear vibration that you are offering your reality. Since manifestation is always taking place in the lives of humans, the key to remember is to observe where you place your focus and your vibrational attention.

This observation will clearly show exactly what has been the focus and what has been the emotional vibration that has been offered by anyone into their reality. Most focus on what they "do not" want to unfold in their lives and reality, rather than focusing on the delicious unfolding of dreams and goals. To this extent, every human is creating their personal experiences and drawing to them what they hold in their vibrational field.

The mass conscious grid holds the patterns of fear, worry, stress, and powerlessness. It is the evolution of each human to recognize that this grid does not belong to them. This grid of limitation, of fear, of mistrust and powerlessness is part of the matrix of the planetary hologame, simply that.

Once the individual human recognizes this illusion, these programmed beliefs, they can certainly and consciously make a shift to create and allow a different result. Each human is a multidimensional starbeing with the incredible ability which molds and sculpts their very existence.

In this hologame on your planet, humans have been taught they are at the effect of events; they do not have the ability or the skills to shift their lot in life. They are taught to vibrate, hold the pattern and hold the thoughts/emotions of unworthiness, impotence, lack and fear.

Humans are rarely taught or made aware of their incredible authority, their omnipotence, their personal power to bring into reality and manifest their highest vision and dream.

This is changing, this is shifting, this is the evolution of the human spirit awakening. Everyone is experiencing this change and this shift in how they view their reality. One by one each human is claiming their mastery, claiming their authority and stepping into their personal sovereignty.

They are recognizing the truth that they are responsible, they hold the power to make an incredible difference in what they experience in the day-to-day unfolding in their lives. Joy, gratitude and appreciation are the keys to this power. It is all vibrations.

One by one
each human is claiming their mastery,
claiming their authority and
stepping into their personal sovereignty.

MESSAGE 48
WAKE UP

Humans are being invited to recognize, accept and honor their multidimensional selves.

It does not serve you or others to continue playing at a low vibration and frequency. It might be familiar and it is certainly a habit well learned, however every human is being pressed to expand into their own magnificence.

Humanity is being confronted with all issues and all the patterns of limited thought and action. This is occurring on the personal scale and the global scale.

Each individual starhuman is facing their believed limitation. Each individual starhuman is facing their patterns, habits, shadows and demons. These habits and patterns are being magnified to the level of extreme discomfort. There is a belief that growth only comes through discomfort or pain.

The energy that is being radiating from the galaxy and bathing humanity is a high vibration; this energy is stirring up all that is a low, dense, slow frequency.

You personally, and humanity at large, have the opportunity to observe where you are holding limited thought patterns and emotional defensive patterns that are vibrating at the low, dense, slow frequencies. When your physical, mental, and emotional states are uncomfortable, that is a red flag, a sign post that is your celestial self pointing the finger to where there is resistance and an energetic blockage. Release these old patterns of limitation in thoughts and feelings.

You have the assistance and support from the realms of truth, love and Light. It is your responsibility to ask for this assistance. Honor yourself and make the conscious shift into positive patterns of unlimited flow.

It depends on your level of discomfort and pain and how long you will continue to allow yourself to experience this restricted flow of divine energy. It is your resistance that is causing your pain. WAKE UP. Your playing small does not serve the higher good.

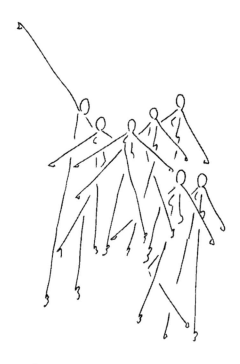

Use consciousness raising tools to make the shift in your energy signature. There is much to do to transform and uplift mass consciousness into the realms of truth. Each human must realize that they hold a key piece in this transformation and that it is their responsibly to release all that limits them at the personal level.

One by one, humanity will begin to vibrate at a pure frequency of LOVE. Each human has a part to play. Each human has certain limited patterns and painful experiences only they can transform. Love yourself free of imagined limitation. Learn to reside in your holy heart, holding steady a vibration of joy, gratitude and appreciation.

Honor yourself
and make the conscious shift
into positive patterns of unlimited flow.

MESSAGE 49
MULTIDIMENSIONAL SOVEREIGNTY

Each moment is an incredible event, yet humans fall into the complacent vibration of sameness, numb to the wonders, magic and synchronicity of their lives. Each moment is a personal connection with the divine.

When you stay in the present moment, conscious in your own magnificence, viewing events with joy, gratitude and appreciation there is a flow, a connection to the higher matrix, the divine weaving, in which all things are possible. It is through the heart portal that this higher matrix is available.

Gratitude opens the channel and you step into each NOW fresh and new. Humans have a tendency to bring the past into each NOW and that shifts the dynamics. The past will only recreate itself, slightly different in frequency, but a reflection of the same.

Each NOW that is honored offers the threshold, the gateway, the portal to your divine manifesting, your divine flow in which grace is your companion. In this state of grace you are offering the collective a pure frequency that transforms everything it touches.

The hearts and minds of the earth dweller are awakening. This reality, this hologame, is a dense energy matrix woven in such a manner that it keeps you engaged, focused, and addicted. Imagine, that the hologame you call your life which keeps you locked into a certain mindsets and actions, is only one program. This hologame is like one of your television programs.

Part of your service is being actively engaged in this hologame which is all about the transformation of energy. Each moment offers the opportunity for the conscious release of any limiting thoughts or emotions. When the discordant vibrations of thought or emotions are held in the space and consciousness of the heart, transformation happens.

The hearts of many humans are energetically shut down, because of the emotions stored in the heart. The personal pains of rejection, abandonment, betrayal, or the loss of loved ones can be changed. It is the conscious willingness that allows this to occur. Each time a discordant emotion is shifted to a more loving or understanding vibration, it can be offered as a gift to the collective.

When the energetic and conscious work is been done to release any personal regrets, past sorrows, or old emotional memories held in the heart, the heart is healed and becomes a true chalice of transformation.

Practice powerful alchemical exercises. In a dedicated moment, imagine some aspect of the collective pain; breath it into your heart and breathe it out transformed. Stay in your heart and in the NOW offering both your joy and gratitude from the awareness of your multidimensional sovereignty.

Gratitude opens the channel and you step into each NOW fresh and new.

MESSAGE 50
COLLECTIVE SHADOW

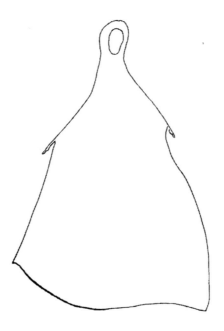

Great changes are occurring. Some are subtle, others occur as a loud struggle. You can observe these different aspects around the world.

There are tremendous challenges and frequencies of hatred, fear and chaos. A large section of humanity is numb, too sensitive to handle the intense frequency of devastation and deception. They feel helpless, unaware of their true power.

Now a wellspring of conscious beings is stepping into true power, aware that they can and do make a difference.

Remember that the shadow of humanity dwells in the consciousness of each person. This shadow aspect of one's self is pushed down, denied and projected. No one wants to think of themselves as prejudiced, judgmental, hate filled, or angry.

No one wants to believe that they could kill another or cause suffering and pain. Yet these very frequencies dwell energetically in the hidden recesses of everyone's psyche to some degree. These qualities of behavior have been programmed, patterned and are activated by fear.

When fear rises up, all these suppressed emotional behaviors are activated. Then there is the illusion of justification in judging another, mocking another, killing another. The shadow of oneself is to be loved free. The insecurities, the pre-programmed beliefs of differences, the collective dysfunction is being pushed to the surface of the collective matrix.

Those who are aware, awakening, and embracing their shadow-selves, are conscious that they are multidimensional beings living in this programmed illusion. They are disconnecting the circuits that trigger the shadow emotions.

They take personal responsibility for the creation of their experiences. When the experience is unpleasant they look within for the cause rather than project the experience or the blame outward.

This evolution of consciousness is swelling, touching the hearts and minds of many. Those who read these words understand and are awakening from the pattern.

The shadow of oneself
is to be loved free.

Message 51
Addictive Emotions

We want to remind you of the importance of maintaining the emotions of joy, gratitude and appreciation.

These are challenging times upon your planet. As an agent of change, a being of Light, you and all others will be most effective in bringing about transformation and change by holding a clear, pure vibration of joy, gratitude and appreciation.

It is important for your well-being, your health, and your ability to connect with your Divine Essence. It is important to recognize when you are vibrating at a low, dense, heavy emotion of fear, anger, sadness, frustration and worry, in order to shift that reality as quickly as possible. It is important for you to make this shift in each moment.

Remember, when you are operating at the frequency of these low, dense emotions, you are automatically plugged into the mass consciousness grid that matches these feelings.

When you allow your emotions to match the mass consciousness grid, you can easily be discouraged and swept away with a sense of being overwhelmed when vibrating at these low frequencies. These dense emotions are the most familiar to you and the easiest to fall into. They are the most prevalent vibrations on earth.

There is an addictive nature to these emotions. The body/brain recognizes the chemical reaction within and this triggers old mental programs, old past experiences, and hurts. Every aspect of your system becomes engaged, with all defensives activated. You are on automatic, easily manipulated by current events.

You are linked to the mass grid/matrix of fear, anger, guilt, worry, frustration, and a feeling of powerlessness. These emotions are holding the evolution of your planet in a lock down. There are those invested in keeping mass consciousness in these easily manipulated states of emotions.

In this game of evolution, this game of transformation, the most valuable skill is the mastery of evoking, sustaining and maintaining high emotional vibrations of joy, gratitude, and appreciation, as well as love. They are your power. Find and focus on the smallest things in your life that you can appreciate and express your gratitude for.

When you are operating at
the frequency of low, dense emotions,
you are automatically plugged into
the mass consciousness grid
that matches these feelings.

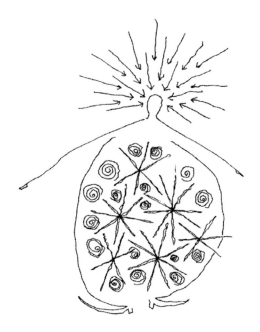

MESSAGE 52
EMOTIONAL ADDICTIONS

*E*veryone has their own set of unconscious programs in which they automatically respond to the events in their lives.

Look at your life and ask yourself what emotion or behavior you might be addicted to. Are you attached to drama? Are you playing out a victim or martyr role? Are you attached to a state of mind in which nothing works? Are you holding on to financial limitations?

Observe without judgment everything in your reality. Take an aspect of your life and look at the pattern from the intention of understanding and releasing. Ask yourself if there was an emotional addiction, what would it be? Know that in the asking the answer will be revealed.

Once you have observed your dysfunctional addictions, it is now a matter of intention and celebration to shift that pattern at every opportunity. It becomes a playful, conscious game of discovery and expansion. We are in a time of great accelerating transformation in which these automatic responses can be discovered, disconnected and deleted.

All multidimensional humans are being invited into the awareness of who they are and the service they offer from their most magnificent self.

Observe the challenges being attracted into your life. These challenges are your greatest gift, for they hold the key, the puzzle piece, to your dysfunctional programs and patterns. With clear intent and gentle observation of ego self, notice and recognize the limiting patterns. Is it your health, wealth, happiness or joy that you are limiting?

Be kind with this search. Ask assistance from your multidimensional awareness; know you are being supported in the clearing of these limitations and the restoring of your true cosmic magnificence.

You are one with the energy fabric of humanity and the universe. When you heal or transform some energy pattern in your circuits, this transformation is available to the entire matrix. You are a transformer.

Take one aspect of your life
and look at the pattern
from the intention of
understanding and releasing.

MESSAGE 53
EGO/MANAGER

Many humans believe that this third dimension reality is all that there is. Most are born, live and die totally unaware of the multitude of realities that they move through each day.

Life is a hologame. The experience you have while in your physical body is only one aspect of who you are. This aspect is important because it offers the opportunity to experience duality, positive and negative. Duality is generated from ego. In the illusion of separation, it is duality which acts as anchor to this illusionary reality. Duality creates the struggle, and the struggle keeps the individual in a level of denseness, in which the ego rules.

Imagine that your ego is only your manager — not the owner, just the manager. However, like most managers, after years of caring for and making all the decisions based on duality your manager/ego believes it is in charge. Now the owner (your divine awareness) returns and wants to run the business (your life), but the ego does not want to lose its control.

Many individuals struggle between the ego self and the higher, aware self. This might be the entire experience of their lifetime — this power struggle between the two. The higher, aware self is gently, lovingly, merging with the aspect you call ego. This is the evolution taking place on your planet, the total merging of the aware multidimensional self fully embodied in physical form, aware of anchoring total balance in the field of duality.

It is in the energy field of balance within that you can become aware of the numerous realities and dimensions in which you travel and dwell. This life is only one of them.

Most of your time is spent in the struggle of duality and all the emotional, mental, and physical aspects that this belief creates. This is busy work, it is polishing the stone. It is the learning.

There comes a time in your growth, your development, your evolution in which you realize it is you and you alone who creates the belief in struggle. When that awareness come to you, the shift, the transformation, and the growth is tremendous.

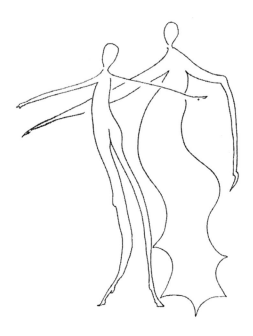

Imagine that your ego
is only your manager—
not the owner, just the manager.

Message 54
Ego Manager Part II

The ego keeps you focused in the third dimension. As you become aware of this, you acknowledge the ego role, which has been the manager of your life. However, YOU, the multidimensional self, now have a very active part, an evolved, conscious, active part.

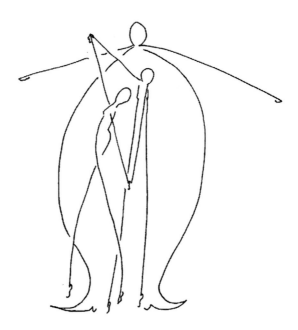

As your multidimensional aspect becomes fully present in your awareness, you gradually realize and recognize that you can move and experience many realities, timeframes and dimensions with ease and delight.

This is the great and grand awakening that is happening upon your planet. More and more beings are becoming aware of the many levels, layers, and realities in which they interface and affect in each moment.

These dimensions overlap and interact. They are woven into the fabric of all. As a multidimensional being, these dimensions, energy fields, and matrices are very real and very visible. It is much like awakening from a dream.

While in a dream, you believe it is real. Yet when you awaken, you observe that it is a dream. You are now awakening from your dream into the multi-dimensions in which your true self dwells and plays.

It is an energy field in which thoughts manifest instantly. It is a reality in which you can travel to any timeframe, any hologame you can imagine. It is a reality that is fluid.

Begin this day being conscious of at least one other reality. Allow yourself to come to the still point within, the balance place within, and then allow yourself to observe what you sense or feel. Relax into this process of discovery.

Like a child's game of hide and seek, begin to be aware of the other realities that have appeared hidden. Notice your beliefs about your physical reality, soften them when they are discovered, and allow other realities, other energy fields, to become visible.

There are energies all around you at all times that you can become sensitive to and interact with from a conscious, multidimensional state of being. Practice this.

While in a dream, you believe it is real. Yet when you awaken, you observe that it is a dream.

When you experience "fear" in the moment...
grab it before it hides...
expose it...
express it and love it free.

MESSAGE 55
FEAR

When the human experiences fear... they drop into a place where they are operating on automatic.

It is "fear" that allows a human to be manipulated... be it fear of the dentist or fear of death or fear evoked by the evening news. It is in that place of unconsciousness... that mental place of operating on automatic that the mass populace usually vibrates. Fear is the key that triggers imbalanced and unconscious patterns.

Notice when you fear something you are becoming powerless. You are easy to manipulate. You disconnect with your Source. You dropped into unconscious behavior. Fear is the key that unlocked that door. Fear triggers your personal insecurities. Be ever diligent... be ever aware... watch closely what experiences... what thoughts... what images... what words trigger your personal fear.

Be aware of the ways that you divert your feeling of fear... the ways you distract yourself... notice the tools you have learned to keep the feelings or vibrations of fear at an unconscious distance

When you experience "fear" in the moment... grab it before it hides... expose it... express it and love it free. "Fear" keeps you from staying in the NOW.

So when you recognize your personal "fears"... deactivate them. You can use your tools of sound... of expression... of sharing... of exploring why the "fear" is there. Where did it come from? How long have you hid it? You can process your "fear" lovingly, consciously, and as you do, you are more available to yourself... you are more available to others. You are more connected to your Source.

MESSAGE 56
ENERGY MATRIX

Humans rarely stay fully present in this physical dimension, they move from one dimension and time frame to another. When they move from one dimension or timeframe to another, they leave an energy trail, a trace or their scent of emotional vibration.

Children are able to shift their awareness from one dimension to another rather quickly. They are not aware they are leaving the physical body. They just naturally travel. They are especially adept at leaving any uncomfortable life situation.

When they leave an uncomfortable situation, they bring an energy trace of those feelings of abuse or trauma with them and they implant those uncomfortable feelings, these emotional vibrations in the other dimension or timeframe.

So many life traumas and family dynamics leave an energy trace which textures or colors the energy of the timeframe or dimension in which they were carried out.

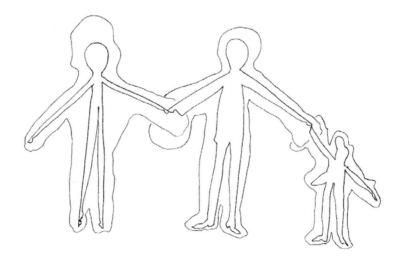

Let us use this example to give you a clear picture and explain this. Imagine a large house with many rooms; each room is a different dimension. If a child has a trauma or experiences some physical, mental or emotional pain, they have a tendency to remove their awareness or consciousness.

They take themselves to a different dimension. So, in this imaginary example of each room being a different dimension, they leave an energy trail. They might store the painful experience or perceived trauma in the back bedroom or the basement or attic.

As an adult, when you are processing your past pain, you must journey from one room to another, releasing the painful trauma, or you must journey from one dimension to another and untangle and release the emotional/mental constructs placed there.

Some traumas are difficult to resolve and release because the person keeps going to the wrong room or wrong dimension to find the source or the seed vibrations of the emotional/mental painful memory and experience.

Use your imagination or visualization to sense or feel the energy trail you might have left in a different timeframe or dimension. Your awareness is your freedom. When you discover these emotional trails, these energy trails, you can gently, lovingly reclaim them and transform the painful energy pattern you left behind.

This type of healing transforms and uplifts you as well as the whole. There are healers from many different timeframes/ dimensions that are here to serve and assist the willing ones to do this service work.

Your awareness is your freedom.

Message 57
Shadow Shapes

The physical reality in which you are embodied has much beauty and wonder. It offers the opportunities to express gratitude and appreciation. From our perspective your physical reality is patterns of light vibrations. Humans have the physical equipment that allows them to see and observe the patterns of light vibrations as solid.

This is called the "illusion". You see the tree outside your window — it appears solid. You could climb this tree in its solidness. You are well aware of the accumulation of leaves which drop from this tree. They are also solid. They have form, texture, shape, and weight. If you cut this tree down, the wood that you could burn would provide warmth. It is a solid, dense, very slow vibrational energy.

The vibrational patterns, the template, the design of this tree are all held in place on the sixth dimension. Remember as a child when you would make shadow shapes upon the wall with the light? It is similar to that concept. Your fingers created the shape of the dog or bird and the light behind your hand created the shadow on the wall.

The physical realities that feel solid and appear real in the third and fourth dimensions are held in place by the reflection of divine intent in the sixth dimension. Remember everything, everything is vibration.

Just as there are vibrations of sound that are vibrating too fast or too slow for your ears to hear, there are light vibrational patterns that are moving so fast your eyes cannot see the vibrations.

Spirit embodied in the human form is restricted by beliefs in limitations. The human body was designed to operate, maneuver and manage the energetic signatures of the third and fourth dimensions.

Spirit, divine mind, your multidimensional self, has waited for you to become aware and dwell in your expanded consciousness, anchored in the physical realms.

A multidimensional human has the capacity to see and sense the shadow shapes on the wall as well as seeing and sensing the hand that is making the pattern and the awareness that they are the light which shines on the hand that makes the shadow.

This elevated awareness allows you to either shift the light or change the patterns or shadow shapes that the hand is making.

There will come a time you will see the tree, and see the energy vibrations resonating from the tree and sense how the tree is touching and weaving into your matrix. This awareness will expand to include the stars.

Awareness allows you to change
the patterns or shadow shapes.

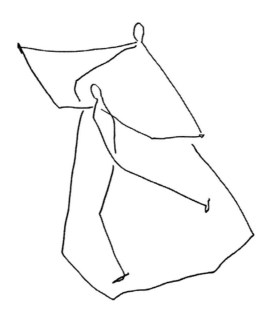

You are awakening
and becoming aware that
you are more than your mind,
your thoughts, and your beliefs.

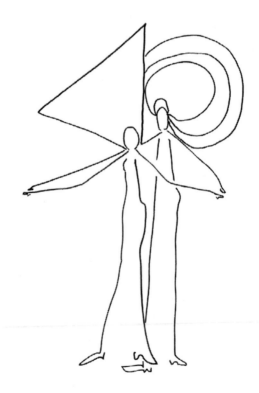

MESSAGE 58
MIND COMPUTER

We remind you that your mind is not who you are. You are Divine Essence.

Your mind is a tool, an awesome tool which allows you to interface with this reality, yet it is only a tool.

Become aware of your mind from the place of observer. It is the observer within who appreciates the sunrise, or thrills at the deer running across the meadow.

The mind is a valuable, necessary aspect of operating in this reality. Your mind is one of the most highly developed computers, capable of incredible tasks, with huge capacity for memory and programs.

This mind computer usually operates on automatic. It will respond from any given program in the system which protects and maintains the well-being and survival of the human. These automatic programs have been installed into your thinking and belief system by others, by our parents, your teachers, and your society.

These programs or beliefs are installed on an emotional frequency and are activated by that same or similar frequency. Once your programs or beliefs have been triggered, the body/chemicals/reaction all responds.

You are now once again engaged in the same or similar response. These similar responses are activated from a place of fear; fear of loss, fear of rejection, fear of harm, fear of death.

Recognize you are awakening and becoming aware that you are more than your mind, your thoughts, and your beliefs. You are more than even your ego.

Staying awake and aware
lifts one's vibrational frequency,
which stops the automatic responses.

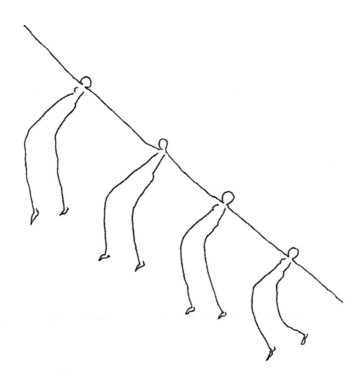

MESSAGE 59
MIND COMPUTER PART II

Many, many humans never realize that they are more than their minds. They are on automatic. They are born, the emotional programs within are installed, and they never question their beliefs or their reactions to these programs. They believe it is their behavior. It is just who they are.

These beings are easily manipulated and controlled, especially by the media, the movies, and games of violence. The body becomes addicted to the chemicals produced when the human is frightened or excited or stimulated in some way.

NOW, at this time, there are those of you who are awakening and becoming conscious.

A human who is conscious uses the incredible abilities of the mind to create new ways of being, new ways of seeing this reality, and new ways of responding to reality.

Here is the tricky part: the old patterns are woven deep into the matrix of society. They are an aspect of mass consciousness. They are strong in their frequency, and are skilled triggers that activate limiting, fearful beliefs and a sense of powerlessness.

It is a moment-to-moment process of staying awake and aware to lift one's vibrational frequency, which stops the automatic responses.

We offer you the reminder to raise your frequency. Your emotions are the key. When you vibrate the frequency of joy, gratitude, and appreciation as well as the master frequency of love, you are in a state of wakeful consciousness. You are heart connected. You are connected to the open channel of guidance and inspiration. You attract and allow more positive life giving energy into your field.

Message 60
Agent of Change

What is happening to the mass consciousness on your planet is that the minds and hearts of everyone are being bathed with unprecedented energy from the galaxy – from the sun, moon and stars.

This energy is triggering the DNA codes, calling individuals to awaken from their unconscious slumber and step fully into their magnificence as beings capable of transforming the denseness of the personal and collective fear.

It is important for each being to train their self; to lift themselves up into the higher emotional vibrations, to reach for feelings of joy, gratitude, and appreciation. These emotions will be your life raft, your buffer, your shield and your safety in times to come.

We encourage you that no matter what—we repeat, that no matter what is happening in the outside world—that you will be wise to maintain an open, expanded state of mind.

The emotions of joy, gratitude, and appreciation will actually buffer and protect you. They will lift you up above the events that are unfolding on your planet. Maintaining a high vibration will be a key to the connection that others will need to link up with.

Your planet is undergoing an evolutionary shift, and the old dense energy—the dense, heavy vibrations of fear, anger, and powerlessness... is being pushed to the surface in all situations, from the individual as well as the collective.

Remember, no one is responsible for how you feel. It is your responsibility as a divine agent of change. Each individual is responsible for the emotions that they offer to the collective.

Do all that is within your power to shift your feelings, one vibration, one frequency, one thought and one emotion at a time. When you offer an energy field of joy, gratitude and appreciation you are open to your internal divine guidance.

You are vibrating at a pure, high frequency above the chaos and you will inspire others to match the frequency you resonate.

Each individual is responsible
for the emotions that they
offer to the collective.

Each human has "codes" in their DNA
that are dormant... not activated...
much like a baby who is born
with the seeds of their own offspring within...

Message 61
DNA

Humans are multidimensional... humans are coded to many realities. Each human has "codes" in their DNA that are dormant... not activated.

Much like a baby who is born with the seeds of their own offspring within... those seeds are dormant until the baby has matured in age and certain hormonal changes within the physical body has taken place... then the 'seeds of reproduction' are ready. The human being is "coded" for various stages of development to happen at certain times... most everyone is aware of the physical changes that take place from baby to adult.

What remains much a mystery to your scientists are the triggers that tell the physical body to begin a certain stage of development. What aspect of the physical body is responsible for the stages of growth, development and maturing?

It is the DNA that carries the "code triggers" that activate each stage. The DNA is the entire operating program of the human.

Humanity is in the process of an evolutionary shift. The dormant codes in the DNA are being switched on... this is activating a new level of knowing within each person.

Humanity is linked to
the stars and beyond.

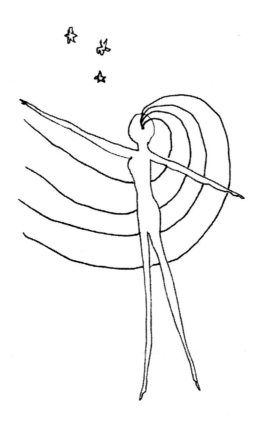

MESSAGE 62
DNA PART II

The main DNA codes that are being triggered at this time within humanity are the awareness and the total sensation of oneness with all.

As more humans are awakening from the numb unconscious illusion of powerlessness and fear... the world is experiencing a global shift.

People are moving from the grid of fear, separation and manipulation into the conscious state of mind, owning their personal power and responsibility in the global and galactic transformation as a part of the divine whole as a multidimensional being.

FEAR, frustration and stress keep the DNA from expanding and the strands from unwinding. These emotions cause the DNA to switch off, then the information these codes carry are unavailable.

The key is the awareness of how your energy/actions/ thoughts/words affect the whole. Holding a pure frequency of joy, gratitude and appreciation allows the DNA to relax and open. As more humans recognize truth... it begins to trigger other "sleepers" to awaken.

There are great forces at work here... humanity is linked to the stars and beyond.

Humans are awakening to their roles and responsibility of this planet... your earth.

Humans are awakening to their role and responsibility of being galactic citizens.

Humans are realizing
they are multidimensional.
They are interactive in other realities.

MESSAGE 63
DNA PART III

Your DNA is interactive with your thoughts/emotions/ beliefs. Your DNA is interactive with others. Your DNA is interactive with the energy of the universe.

Galactic power surges, solar flares, vibrating a pure frequency of joy/gratitude/ appreciation all contribute to the triggering... the switching on of more and more of the dormant aspects of your DNA.

Human beings are made up of complex fields of energy...all interweaving, moving, shifting and changing moment-to-moment.

These energy fields interact with other humans beyond words or consciousness. More is shared and communicated on the subtle energy grids of each person than words spoken. When two people come together there is a total interface... a mixing as it were of the energy fields of each one... volumes of information is available to both.

As the DNA codes and programs are activated... this awareness of being in more than one reality at any moment will become the norm.

Humans are realizing they are multidimensional. They are interactive in other realities. They are more magnificent than they can ever imagine. They can read emotional history and experiences in one in breath. They can process data and information on another level while staying focused on this reality and dimension.

Message 64
Heart Portal

The heart is the thinking organ of your human form, it is truly in command. The energetic field of the heart matrix is far stronger and more expanded than that of the energetic matrix of the brain. Your mentors and avatars have been teaching this for lifetimes.

Human beings long ago learned to close or protect their heart circuit. This is the main dysfunction on your planet and the main source of dis-ease.

When the heart circuit is protected there is an energetic loop. There is a thought shield that filters or monitors the coming in or the going out of energy in a more guarded manner. The human being has allowed the brain, the programs, and beliefs to monitor and guard the heart center. These programs/beliefs close and numb your responses to the messages and guidance coming from and going to this heart center.

These beliefs about protecting the heart center are passed down energetically from parents to child. A child learns from the unspoken as well as the spoken messages about being hurt, or loving freely and easily, what feels safe or unsafe, who to trust or not trust.

There are the wounds passed down from generation to generation. There are the wounds within the family dynamics of this lifetime. There are the wounds that each human being has personally experienced while in this embodiment.

The heart center is your portal. It is your gate. It is important for humanity to begin to heal the wounds that their heart carries. It is essential to healing the planet, one heart beat at a time, one human being at a time.

This is the responsibility for each and every person on the personal level, genetic level and global level, to heal the wounded patterns within the heart matrix. Humanity is stepping into an entirely new paradigm in which the thinking heart will be the honored, whole, and connected to the other heart matrices.

The heart portal was designed to serve as the gateway to the stars, allowing the energy to flow from divine source out into your reality.

The important tools in healing and harmonizing your heart portal are the vibrations of joy, gratitude and appreciation. It is the power of these vibrations which allows the heart center/heart portal to heal from all the wounds carried.

It is the service work each human being is asked to give for the wholeness and healing of the heart center of humanity, for when human beings live from an open and healed heart they know and feel their connected with each other.

Beliefs about protecting the heart center are passed down energetically from parents to child.

Message 65
Struggle versus Flow

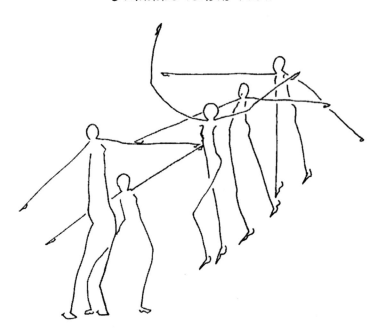

One of the important masteries and skills you bring to all your experiences while embodied is how fully conscious you are in each NOW.

It does not matter what you are doing or with whom you are doing it, the key is to be in the moment, fully filled with your joy, gratitude, and appreciation. It is not what you do but how you do each moment.

Everyone longs to discover the place of harmony and the gentle flow of events. When you experience struggle and stress this adds a level of disharmony to the activity and the seeming chaos. Once the energy dynamics of struggle and stress are engaged it takes conscious skill to change and transform the pattern.

The belief that everything is a struggle, a challenge, a strain is strong in mass consciousness. This is an illusion and a learned pattern.

There is a mental state of mind and an emotional state of being in which we invite you to maintain. When your awareness is in the present moment of NOW and you are holding an energetic stance of a high vibration, no matter what you are doing, there will be a flow, a grace, and an ease.

The illusion of struggle, stress and strain creates low frequencies. These states of mind vibrate/radiate in the third dimension. They are a part of the matrix of lock-down.

Many humans are aware they are multidimensional beings playing in a hologame here on planet earth. This hologame board offers the illusion of limitations.

The illusion of limitations is strong, it is well maintained, and it is encouraged and enforced by the media, the leaders, and the old third dimensional paradigm.

The beliefs of limitation are given to each human upon arrival by parents and society. Many humans never question or discover that they are truly powerful creators. They exist and live their lives with a poverty of consciousness.

There is an evolution, a transmutation that is happening in the hearts and minds of scores of humans. This evolution of consciousness expands into the truth of the unlimited self, aware of their lives in multi-realities.

The awareness of staying in a high vibration of joy, gratitude and appreciation allows you to stay in the fifth dimension where synchronicities, miracles, and divine connection allow for a graceful flow of events and activities to take place. Practice these skills today and notice how events unfold with more fluidity and less struggle.

Many humans never question or discover
that they are truly powerful creators.

MESSAGE 66
PORTAL OF NOW

We actually marvel at the busyness and various and diverse ways humans use their time, energy and focus. In this physical reality the goal is to understand, manage and transform energy that is dense and limiting, to bring the purest consciousness to everything.

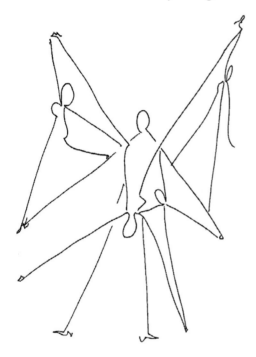

Most humans perform their tasks and activities mentally absent from the action. They are thinking of something else. Their mind is traveling to the past and to the future. Rarely do they stay fully present in the NOW.

This is especially true of mundane tasks, repeated over and over, day in and day out. There is an automatic behavior that performs the task and the human is not fully aware or conscious of the energy or any difference in the grid or field. By not being fully in the NOW they don't bring their consciousness of light to the moment.

Most humans stay in the activities of the mind. They allow the mind free rein of the day and the energy that flows through the body. They are spendthrifts in regards to the divine transformational energy that is given upon each breath, unaware of the power they have to shift any activity they are involved with.

They complete one task in order to complete another, like a duty totally absent of any feeling or heart connection. It is time to develop the keen awareness that no matter what you are doing in your daily life, it is affecting the entire universal matrix. We repeat — anything you are doing affects the matrix.

The mundane task of paying your bills can be a moment of divine transformation for you and for the energy grid, if you bring your full presence into the activity. You can infuse this simple action with your light and your blessings with such intent that it will be felt by others involved in the process.

Step into the sacred awareness that you have the power to infuse toxic, low vibrations with uplifting, transforming cosmic vibrations at all times. Practice bringing this incredible divine light into everything that you do.

The more you bring your consciousness into the NOW and stay in your heart frequency, the quicker your reality will shift and transform. It is the dwelling on the past and the projecting into the future that keeps you from dancing in the NOW.

The NOW moment is where the power is. The NOW moment is a place of sacred balance. The NOW moment offers a clear, pure portal for manifestation.

Develop the keen awareness that
no matter what you are doing in your daily life,
it is affecting the entire universal matrix.

Message 67
NOW is a Portal

Remember "Be here NOW." NOW is a Portal. It is one thing to have this as a concept, an interesting awareness in the mind and it is another thing to practice it moment to moment.

One aspect of your planetary matrix and planetary hologame includes the belief about time. Time only exists because you think it does. You allow time to rule and control your life. Time is fluid and flexible and acts according to your beliefs.

Your personal programming and the program of the hologame make time solid and gives time the illusion of being real. This concept is a difficult one to comprehend especially when you are coming from the lock-down matrix of this "timeframe."

Much stress comes from projecting your consciousness into the future, energizing it with worry, concerns, and fears. Holding onto it and dragging it into every NOW. In this hologame it is important to plan, however once the plan is in place, let it go. Ask yourself often, am I in the NOW or in the past or the future? Observe and watch where you place your attention.

Remember, if your thoughts are always comparing the past to the NOW, you are still in the memories of the past, you are not fully present in the fresh new moment. Often you flavor your NOW with worries of the future, again this shifts the moment.

The NOW is your point of power where you create anew. In the present moment you can make clear intentions, and hold a clear vision of a future event. You are setting the framework and planning for a future outcome. This is good work. Once that is complete, release it, allow and trust your creative intent to bring you the results of your clear vision.

With conscious awareness you can stay in your NOW and from the NOW plan or schedule appointments or events. Once you have arranged for that future event release the energy and return your focus to the new NOW and its tasks. So just relax, and practice returning your awareness to the Now as often as possible.

By staying in the present moment, you will become aware that each NOW is a timeless portal. You will gently begin to notice time will shift for you. It will stretch, it will wrinkle, it will fold and it will disappear.

Become aware that
each NOW is a timeless portal.

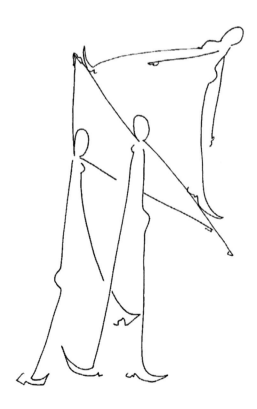

MESSAGE 68
FULLY IN THE NOW

This is your key... in all your activities and projects and mundane tasks, practice bringing your full consciousness to the moment.

Allow all your senses to be involved: the sights, the smells, the textures. There will come a moment when you are dancing with each NOW that you will realize the translucent quality of staying fully in the present moment.

There is magic, an alchemical power available to each starhuman who learns to ride the wave of energy that is creating all the NOW's. It is a skill, it is a game, and it is an invitation.

Practice today as you go about your mundane tasks to anchor divine energy into the moment. Practice returning to your full awareness. Practice stepping out of your habitual thoughts that run your unconscious activities, practice being fully in the present moment.

The place to start is the heart center. When you place your awareness in your heart you will naturally dwell in the NOW.

It is the mind that likes to play in the realms of past and future. It is the mind that dwells in the game of what if's and if only's, of regrets and sorrows. It is the mind that entertains fear and hatred. It is the programs of the mind that keeps each multidimensional starhuman locked in the illusion of limitations.

This is the highest and grandest service you can offer others. It is your full divine presence. It is your full divine presence in the NOW.

There is no time! Time is a part of this hologame, part of this illusion, and time is a function of the mind. Time keeps you locked out of the NOW.

By practicing staying in the NOW, you step out of the illusion of time. It is a learned skill and it is much easier than you would imagine. Remember, any experience when you felt total joy and overwhelming gratitude, you were fully in the NOW.

Bring your full consciousness to each moment and you will be embraced by your joy and gratitude. This joy and gratitude will bubble up from your sacred heart and radiate out to all. Then every activity and every encounter will be uplifted into the realms of light and love. You will begin to live in the sacred alchemical portal of the NOW.

Staying in the NOW,
you step out of the illusion of time.

MESSAGE 69
ARTIFICIAL FREQUENCIES

It is important to remain consciously connected to this planet. Your earth has a magnetic field, rhythm and frequency which have a significant affect on your personal well-being, wholeness, health and balance.

In the past humans lived closer to the earth and the rhythms. They lived out-of-doors, slept on the ground, farmed the lands, hunted and walked touching the soil. This way of living offered a deep sense of belonging and connectedness to the resonance and vibrations of the planet. Your society at this time is less likely to experience this deep connection with the earth.

Most of the population lives in a world of man-made concrete and asphalt. They are born into a home that is surrounded by buildings. Those in the cities can go days, weeks, months and even lifetimes without a real connection to the earth.

Humans are not connected in a healthy way to the vibrational field of earth. People surround themselves with artificial, discordant vibrations created by man. Everything in your home has a vibration no matter how solid it feels to your touch or seems to your eyes, it is vibrating slowly perhaps, but it is vibrating. These surroundings in the workplace or the home do not support your balance and well-being.

Add another layer to this artificially created matrix—the electronic frequencies from all your appliances, TV, computers, telephones, refrigerators. These are the discordant man-made energy frequencies in which most people live.

Alarmingly, these high frequency energetic grids are increasing and as they do, the populace becomes more chaotic, unbalanced, unwell, and dis-eased.

The personal energy or matrix of the human is sensitive to these energetic grids, these electronic frequencies which are passing through their tissues and their bones, affecting their state of mind, their health, their sense of wholeness and balance.

We invite you to make it a conscious practice to connect with the healing, whole energetic matrix of nature, and what it offers in balance and freshness to your energy. The cohesive frequencies of nature, the vibrations of living trees, plants, stones, lakes, oceans are like whole, alive food to the human energetic field.

If you live in the city you will need to be more creative. Bring living plants into the space, the caring for these living plants offer a simple method to balance the artificial frequencies. Make it a point to find a park or some form of nature and spend time there. This allows your energy body to discharge any unwanted stale energy and to be replenished with a more cohesive, whole, alive, healthy vibration.

You can also sing, move, stretch, dance, look at the beauty of the day and create a flow of joy and gratitude in your personal field.

Make it a conscious practice to connect with the healing, whole energetic matrix of nature.

MESSAGE 70
ONE VIBRATIONAL FIELD

Your human form is only one aspect of who you are. As a human focused in and on this third dimension, it feels real, looks real, yet it is only one perceptive of the multidimensional aspect of the starhuman.

Each dimension is always available, resonating at a different frequency. When starhumans become conscious, other realities and dimensions appear.

Your astronomers continue to discover new planets beyond your known solar system. This is an example that humanity has raised its consciousness enough to allow these 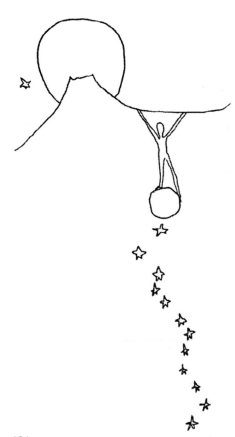 planets to be visible, much like the knowledge of quantum physics and the incredible awareness of energy within the smallest particles, affecting and being effected by our thoughts.

Let's use your human body as an example of the multidimensional levels. You have a dense physical form — the shape, height and weight of your body is what you see reflected in a mirror. But, this is only the outer appearance.

Within the human form are entire galaxies, entire systems, and entire energy fields. Each of these systems functions automatically below your conscious awareness, much like the multidimensional realities outside your body. You are affecting both the inner dimensions within your physical body and the outer dimensions of your reality.

Everything is a reflection. "As Within, So Without. As Above, So Below." This is a true statement by your Einstein.

The nucleus of the atom spins within the cell; it is quantum physics in action. Your thoughts and emotions affect the spin, just as thoughts and emotions of mass consciousness effect the spin of your planet and the stars; the spin of the planet and the stars affect the spin of the atoms within your cells. This is one energetic vibrational field of incredible variations and combinations.

Hold the perspective that you are always operating at a multi-dimensional level within your human form and outside your human form. Allow yourself to become aware of these other realities and dimensions.

Within the human form are
entire energy fields,
entire systems,
and entire galaxies.

MESSAGE 71
LIVING AS ONE CELL

Consider the awareness of your multidimensionality. You are here in a hologame on planet earth, responsible for the physical vehicle in which you dwell, confined by beliefs of the limitations of this reality. You are also connected to the galaxy and respond to the energy matrix offered.

You are able to read the energy of another being, taking in data and interfacing with other beings at all times; exchanging information, ideas, and weavings of energy. You travel through time in a moment—returning to the past, zooming to the future, however, you only touch the time line briefly and usually you touch it with regret or worry.

You have the ability to step into any hologame and experience that reality, with all its taste, smells, feelings and sights, and "live" it so to speak. However, in this current third dimension reality you have mimicked this multidimensional ability with the movies and television.

Use the example of the physical body as a metaphor. Image that within the body, this physical life you are now focused on, your dimension of awareness is only "one cell". Your life, your "NOW" is only one cell. Yet you and the others you interact with are truly multidimensional. The multidimensional self creates, nurtures, and sustains the whole in a very complex, delicate balance.

You as the "one cell" are not aware of all the other tasks or other realities the total body participates in. There is the reality of the bones, the reality of skin, the reality of the heart, the liver, the circulation system—these are all just aspects of the multidimensional reality of the body. There is the brain, the thoughts, the feelings, the memories and on and on. Yet the one cell awareness is not fully conscious of all that continues to take place.

This human life is your focus, yet it is only one cell of your total magnificent multidimensional self. There is much going on at all times that you do not recognize because of your veiled awareness and belief systems. There are frequencies, matrices, and realities that exist in which you are very active. Yet the "one cell" you focus on resists this expansion or does not even know of the others' existence.

Expand your awareness. It is much easier than one might imagine. You do it often, now just recognize when you have shifted.

This human life is your focus,
yet it is only one cell of your total
magnificent multidimensional self.

MESSAGE 72
VIBRATIONAL MATRIX

First let us say that you appear to us as vibrational patterns, weavings of energy, light and sound. These patterns and weaving shift and move in constant flow and fluctuation. Your vibrational matrix gives the appearance of the galaxy in all its expanded wonder.

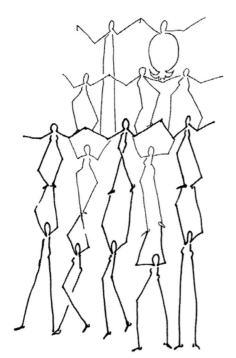

Quantum physics tells you that the human body is mainly space. It is not solid, even though it appears solid and feels solid. It is like outer space; your atoms shine like the stars in your night sky. We are inviting you to stretch into the realms in which you might see your form as we do.

There are some who have the ability to see the vibrational matrix. They can see the energy weavings of color, sound and light. Many can sense, feel or even hear the vibrational matrix of another. This vibrational matrix has many names: aura, charisma, magnetism. This ability to see or hear the vibrational matrix of another will become more common as humans expand into their multidimensional awareness.

Today we would like to share with you what the vibrational matrix contains and how it is formed. Just as the human vehicle is formed in the mother's womb, so begins the energy weavings. Each human form is a collection of vibrations that entwine into energy patterns. This vibrations network is created by the emotions, thoughts and experiences.

All human experiences are translated into this vibrational matrix, this energy fabric. The experiences in this third/fourth dimension are not supportive to the expansion and strengthening of the individual vibrational matrix. The dysfunction and unconsciousness that is commonplace within humanity has created tangles or blockages in the weavings of the energy fields.

These energy tangles slow or block the flow of divine life altogether. The results are a humanity that is dying. It is this vibrational matrix that holds the pattern and weavings for the formation of the human body with all its interrelated and interdependent elements.

Every cell and atom vibrates at a certain rate. The bones, the blood, all the organs, every aspect of the physical form is held in place and created from this vibrational matrix. The physical form matches the vibrational matrix. This is a rather simple way to state an incredible complex concept, however it offers an invitation for more discovery.

Play with this idea and all of its implications. Notice the places in which you are expanded and the places you might have energy tangles. Be playful and joy filled in your discovery of reading your own and others' vibrational matrix.

Each human form is a
collection of vibrations
that entwine into energy patterns.

MESSAGE 73
SIXTH DIMENSIONAL WORK

The seed matrix of each human is an essential to understanding our true nature. It is that which gives origin or form in this reality. It is that which carries the energetic vibrations for each physical form. There is much value and significance in the comprehension and clear awareness of energy matrices.

It is this master matrix, this seed matrix of each human, which holds the divine blueprint. All records, all emotional experiences, all energetic signatures, are intertwined within this energy weaving.

It is within this personal seed matrix, this vibrational matrix, that all physical, mental, emotional and spiritual imbalances can be restored.

Your hospitals and care givers would proceed very differently if the seed matrix or the energy signature of each patient could be read, scanned and recognized. This would be the first and main area of approach in healing and restoring health to the physical body.

Just imagine having the ability to scan this personal energy matrix, see the areas where there is a tangle in the energetic weavings, or a blockage to the flow of divine life, then gently untangling the threads.

Once the original pattern has been restored to the master matrix, the physical body would manifest this rebalance and alignment. The body's divine integrity would be restored. This is truly sixth dimensional (and beyond) healing work.

Vibrational medicine works with the matrix in restoring well-being and health. It is all vibration, remember! Each energy matrix has its own sound frequency or frequencies.

Each human's matrix offers a sound frequency which is in resonance or "in tune" with well-being and aliveness, or is in dissonance and "out of tune" with well-being and aliveness.

There are human beings who have understood this and those who have the ability and awareness to see the energy matrices. This is a natural ability of all humans who step into the realms of their multidimensional selves. This awakening is happening within the consciousness of humans everywhere.

Those who offer and serve with energy work, sound, music therapy, and other vibrational practices are facilitating the untangling of emotional or mental patterns held in the matrix.

Here again, we remind you that energy follows thought and the importance of willingness as well as intention to facilitate this work. Notice today if you are in resonance with your joy, gratitude and appreciation. These vibrations, these feelings, will restore balance and well-being.

Awakening is happening within the consciousness of humans everywhere.

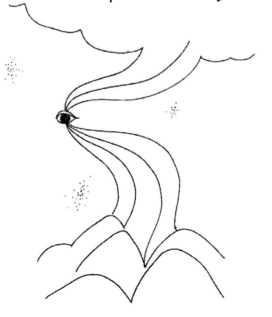

201

Message 74
A Bigger Playground

You are being invited to practice ways of riding the intense energy waves being generated from the stars.

Everything you experience as solid and "real" is vibrations of energy, held or locked in place by belief systems. If you could set aside all the mental programs about your reality you would experience a different reality. There are dimensions and timeframes you can experience and 'travel'.

Imagine a child who is raised in a small house. All their needs are met—they are happy, yet their entire world is the small house. They become an adult, yet never venture out of the small house, believing that the small house is all that exists. They see nothing more—all their beliefs and mental programs tell them that reality is only that one small house.

Then something happens and they are shocked out of their stance and beliefs. They catch a glance of a bigger reality beyond the small house. This is the beginning of expanded awareness.

This is happening on your planet. People are being shocked out of their stance of what's real. It's frightening and fearful and they have a tendency to run back into the small house, with small, safe, limited beliefs about reality.

We are encouraging you to step out the door and embrace the countless realities that are only a frequency or vibration away.

Allow yourself to imagine traveling to the stars. Allow yourself to see energy in its different forms without an overlay of your beliefs. Allow yourself to imagine how music might look or how music might smell rather the just how it sounds. Allow yourself to stretch into a space in which you question your beliefs and how you perceive your life.

Assistance is being given to awaken humanity to the rich tapestry of multi-realities. Reality is a bigger, freer playground. Reality is riding the energy flow. Reality is reading the energy signature of the moment. Reality is expansive.

Increase your personal vibration to a higher resonance. Balance, laughter, joy and gratitude are vibrational tickets that allow you to travel into these new realities of wonder and awe.

Everything you experience
as solid and "real"
is vibrations of energy,
held or locked in place by belief systems.

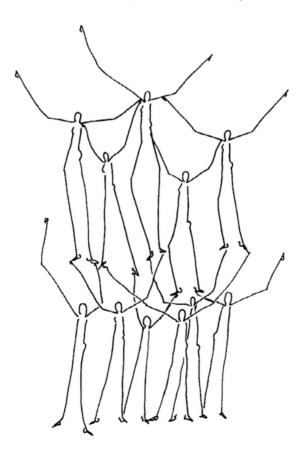

MESSAGE 75
JOURNEY TO OTHER HOLOGAMES

This reality/hologame is only one of many you participate in. As multidimensional starbeings your presence is simultaneously expanded to a multitude of other realities and hologames, which are layered, woven, and nested within each other.

This example will offer some clarity. You are here, perhaps at your desk focused with us and this message. That is one facet of the hologame/reality that you embrace.

You could step out of the hologame, this matrix, and travel to a friend's home and be in an entirely different hologame and matrix. Or you could be in the shopping mall and again it would be a different hologram and different matrix.

Each time you take your presence to a different event or activity, you are shifting the hologame. However in your consciousness, it is just different aspects of your life here on earth.

Now expand this concept to the galactic arena. It is the same. One hologame and reality is your total life here on this planet; however, there are certainly other realities and other planes of existence in which you are fully present, conscious, and an active energy field and vibration in that reality.

All these realities are nested, woven, and layered, just like your current embodiment and current life here on earth.

The key is to your awareness of being at your desk, or being at your friend's house or being at the office or shopping mall. You hold all these activities and all these changes in events and activities as a part of your life.

Your galactic life is the same. You have multidimensional realities, activities, events and hologames in which you participate, and this reality here on earth is only one of those holograms. It feels a bit overwhelming to consider that you are active in a multitude of various realities and timeframes, all of which are happening at once.

Allow this idea to stretch your mental concept, play with this possibility, especially when you have undisturbed time alone. Allow your consciousness and imagination to travel unrestricted and observe what images, feelings, thoughts and experiences occur.

Leave your small judging and doubting mind in a safe place, and play freely like a child of the universe that you are. The galaxy is your total playground.

Practice consciously sending forth a pure frequency of joy, gratitude, and appreciation. These vibrations, these frequencies are your anchor, your ticket, your magic carpet, your protection and your wings in any reality or hologame. Safe, smooth and gentle travels!

This is the awakening time.

Message 76
Time is Elastic

*E*ach individual is confronted with their old third dimensional time beliefs as they move in consciousness to the other dimensions. Humanity has recorded time, history and past events with clocks, calendars, and all manner and methods of measure.

Imagine moving into a new frequency in which time as you have known it does not exist. Imagine an expanded state of consciousness in which what you thought and what you expressed was manifested instantly with no time lag. You would think about something and it would appear before you.

There are those among you who have expressed this concept in many ways. Your story by Richard Bach, Jonathan Livingston Seagull, says it very well; "To fly as fast as thought, to be anywhere there is, you must first begin by knowing that you have already arrived".

You are experiencing the inner conflict of your concepts of time and the realization that you are more than your physical body. You are an unlimited being of expansive states of consciousness.

You can travel time, shift time, honor time, struggle time, collect time, try to hold on to time, or you can relax and embrace the energetic shift that is taking place within your consciousness and the consciousness of all sentient beings.

We are exposing one of your most sacred belief systems and we understand your resistance and your confusion.

We invite you to play with this thing called time. Pretend that you can stretch it, expand it, and mold it to your day and your projects. You are learning to use your conscious mind to create.

So, if you are feeling stress you will only create more stress. If you are feeling time restraints, you create a reality of not enough time.

Make time your friend. It is very elastic and very flexible. Play with it in a new way. Relax into your tasks. Breathe, Laugh, and Lighten Up.

Imagine moving into a new frequency
in which time as you have known it
does not exist.

MESSAGE 77
TIME AS FLUID FLOW

Spacious time lives in the NOW. Your beliefs/programs and your energetic stance of struggle creates time that is rather restrictive.

Time, in your earthly hologame, is a sacred belief. It is firmly anchored in your matrix and in all the programs that operate your mental activities. Most humans have some form of this rigid belief about time, with many rules and countless ways to measure time.

Everyone has experienced time being rather fluid. When doing a job in which you are bored, time seems to move slowly. When you are totally engaged in an activity, time disappears and you wonder "Where did the time go?"

This is your perception of time. Remember energy follows thought. Time follows thought. Your thoughts about time arise from your belief system about time.

As humans, you are engaged with the matrix of time. As a multidimensional being you can and do step out of this earthly limited matrix of time. It is a matter of awareness and practice.

Look at your beliefs and question your beliefs about time. Notice how you worship time, how you covet time, how you wrap your activities in limited time. Notice your struggles and seeming stress that is created from these beliefs. Notice how mass consciousness holds these beliefs about time.

Asking you to look at the matrix of time in a new way is similar to asking a fish about the water in which it swims, or the bird about the air in which it flies. The fish is so enveloped by water and bird is so enveloped by air, they cannot conceive of a different reality.

To understand the concept of time one must first know and investigate just how the energy matrix of time controls and runs their life.

Notice where time stalls for you and where you allow it to flow.

Notice how often you truly stay in the present moment of NOW.

Practice bringing your awareness into each NOW. Notice what you say about time and how you share your limited beliefs about time. "I never have enough time." "Time is running out." "Time is speeding up."

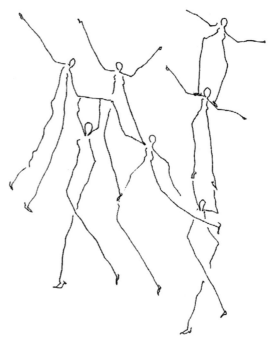

Play with this, allow this to be fun. It does not have to be so serious. Time is not as sacred as you have made it. It is flexible and fluid. Allow yourself to stretch into that unlimited, magnificent energy matrix of NOW.

Acknowledge yourself when you experience time as a new spacious form. Acknowledge when you experience a synchronicity; this is time being fluid.

Remember it is from the NOW
that you can and do step out of time.

MESSAGE 78
MATRIX OF UNLIMITED TIME

Time is fluid — it is not contained in your clocks or the pages of your calendar. Those are tools created for measuring this thing called time. It is important that you continue to investigate and query your own personal time matrix. These are the beliefs that you were given by your family and society and are only programs within your system.

Your personal belief about time is just another agreement that you assumed because it felt solid and everyone said it was solid. In the earthly hologame it is a part of the game rules. Everyone will honor time and give it the power to run the show.

What if time is fluid? How would that effect your day and the participation in your earthly life? Just for a moment, let us imagine that past, present and future are all happening and shifting simultaneously. It is your perception of time that places them in the rigid placement.

Imagine that events in your future could shift the events from your past which would alter your present "NOW". As a multidimensional being this is how you would and could address this concept called time.

As a human locked into the third/fourth dimension, the rigid beliefs and laws that you have been taught about time are just programs in your bio-computer.

The rules of life on the earth plane are arranged around time. We can hear your comments about being late for appointments, waking up on time, catching a plane at a certain time, important dates and events happening at a given time.

Time as you know it here on planet earth is important to recognize and be aware of because it makes playing the game understandable. However, it is not the only recognized system of time in the universe. It is a limited system.

Sense your limited beliefs about time and then begin to allow your consciousness to become more fluid and watch how your perception of time becomes more fluid.

Expand into the matrix of unlimited time, where with just a thought you could and would be anywhere on the timeline. Imagine with just a focused thought you could be present at any event, anywhere, at any time.

Remember, outside this reality, time is fluid. It is with your focused expanded consciousness that you travel time. Play with this concept. Imagine just what you would do if you could travel time. Make it a playful and joy filled experience.

Your personal belief about time
is just another agreement.

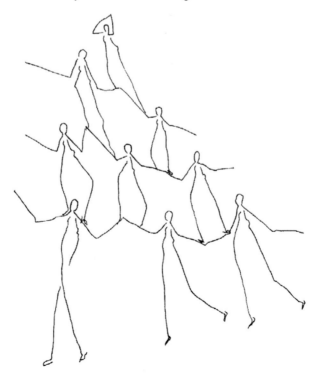

Message 79
Practice Stillness

We will speak to you of stillness, for it is within the moments of stillness that balance is restored.

In the future days as the energy flooding your earth increases, those who walk this timeframe will experience much chaos and the seeming out of balance of daily and global events. It is most important to develop the skill of maintaining your personal balance in the midst of these difficult and changing times.

We invite you to make a practice of stillness, be quiet for a few minutes several times a day. As you practice and use this simple tool, it will become easier and quicker to reach your state of balance. Stillness allows your body/mind/emotions/spirit to realign.

When you notice you are feeling the most stressed, the most harried, that is truly the time to pause, become quiet, and reset. Practice conscious stillness. This practice keeps your circuits open for guidance.

This will become as natural as your breath and you will carry a balanced energy field which will assist you in your personal interface with life experiences and it will assist the global matrix, the global energy field to resonate a state of balance.

Like all things in the hologame, this practice of stillness will shift the whole. Small, simple, dedicated actions infused with joy, gratitude, and appreciation will ripple outward from your life, shifting and transforming all other energy it touches.

You and others who practice conscious stillness will offer an example, a safe harbor, and a balanced frequency for others to entrain and resonate with. Your numbers will increase as you offer balance to the energy fields you interact with in your daily activities.

We encourage you to practice conscious stillness. This exercise will open many more doors of awareness for you and strengthen your connection with your guidance.

It is most important to develop
the skill of maintaining
your personal balance in the midst of
these difficult and changing times.

MESSAGE 80
RITUAL

We offer you the expanded perception of the sacred art of ritual. Rituals open and close an activity — simple.

Rituals can be as basic as a spoken word of acknowledgement of what is taking place, or as elaborate as you can imagine. Each person will find the most comfortable place to bring more ritual into their life, their day and their actions. Rituals and intentions invite a very conscious vibration into your awareness and how you interface with all aspects of reality.

A simple ritual before a meal prepares the mind/body to accept the foods offered. A closing prayer of gratitude, a simple bowed head, completes the act of eating. A ritual created as you shower or bathe has great power to cleanse the energy field as well as the body.

Rituals can be used to create a framework to hold an activity, an event or gathering. There are rituals for release and rituals for bringing forth. Begin to be aware of the rituals you already have in your life. Some you might call habits. Look and see how you can shift and elevate these habits to become spiritual acts.

You can elevate, offer as a higher vibration the simple tasks you perform each day. There are rituals that you can create that honor the stages of each day.

A morning ritual can be as simple as a spoken prayer or you may decide to expand your ritual to include several acts that will consciously enhance this stage of your day. Perhaps you light a candle, say your prayer and bring your awareness fully into your physical form, filling yourself with the energy, the sounds and the gift the morning offers. This is a time for gratitudes, a time for intention, a time to connect.

Then at your noontime... be aware that you have entered another stage of the day... leave behind what is complete from the morning and step into this different rhythm and energy.

Again before your nights sleep, have a ritual to honor the day lived, acknowledging self, releasing all that needs to be released. This is a time of forgiveness and of gratitude.

With conscious awareness and dedicated practice these daily rituals will soon be smoothly woven into your day, adding new dimensions to your life.

Rituals and intentions

invite a very conscious vibration

into your awareness, actions and activity.

Through rituals,
you see your every action as holy,
each and every action becomes sacred.

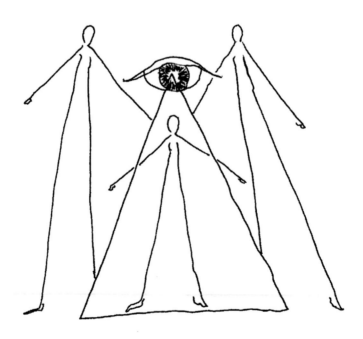

MESSAGE 81
RITUAL PART II

Rituals assist in the full spiritual presence coming forth. There are rituals that you can perform honoring each season of the year. Then the seasonal energy construct you have called forth will flavor the days that follow.

Your body/mind/emotions and spirit will remember the significance of the season, the qualities, and the attributes of this time of the year and will flow more in harmony with it. There are rituals in which you can be aware of the lunar cycles and its movement with your body. You will be able to observe the rhythms, the pull and the pulse.

There are rituals for the stages in your life, as you move through the ages and the seasons of your timeline. By honoring these passages with rituals you are able to step cleanly from one stage into the next.

Creating a ritual that honors the stage you are leaving, completed bringing the lessons and gifts and releasing what is finished. By your conscious actions in this ritual you will embody each stage in your life more fully.

There are rituals that you can perform honoring each season of the year. Then the seasonal energy construct you have called forth will flavor the days that follow.

Through rituals, you see your every action as holy, each and every action become sacred. From the preparation of food to the daily task of cleaning, you bring your full spiritual presence to each activity.

By the act of creating rituals you stay more conscious, more present, and more alive with all that you do, with every action that you take.

MESSAGE 82
OUT OF THE BOX

The dimensions are a matter of frequency and vibration. Humans travel from one dimension to another many times a day. If it is not within their belief system, they are not aware of this and will not recognize this happening. For them it does not exist.

You only see what you believe. Your reality matches your beliefs. That's the tricky part. You look out at your reality and see a certain experience. You see it—it looks real, feels real, and others agree that it's real. Therefore, it must be real.

You continue to gather proof of its realness. You even write books about its realness. You have organizations around its realness. You fight for its realness. It is only real because you are operating in a frequency or belief that makes it real. This is what is termed a locked down reality. Everything strengthens the illusion and strengthens the beliefs of the illusionary realness.

The key is to begin to stretch your beliefs, stretch your knowing. You have a term that is excellent which invites this stretch— Think out of the box.

Notice when your experiences feel limiting. Notice when you are thinking thoughts that do not empower you. Notice when you feel shut down. Notice when you long for more yet feel trapped. Notice when you sense there is something more that could unfold. When that is happening you are touching the sides of your limitation box.

At those moments you can shift the frequency, you can shift your mental vibration and begin to allow another reality to emerge; practice stretching, expanding your way of viewing events. Practice a visualization of being above the events or just outside the event. Change your perspective, your viewpoint, just a little.

Allow the sides of your belief box to expand to include something slightly different, slightly new, something that you "normally" would not even consider a possibility because it would be too far out, too unreal. Remember you see what you believe.

Making connections with other dimensions is just a matter of stepping out of the box, the limited mental or emotional box. It is vibrating at a higher frequency, stepping out of old, limited beliefs and welcoming the awareness of your multidimensional starself.

Allow a softening, a merging of the dimensions, a flow, gentle and smooth shifting frequency and vibration. The golden key is conscious practice of vibrating joy, gratitude and appreciation, moment to moment to moment. These are high frequency vibrations; they allow your box of limited thinking to disappear.

Allow the sides of your belief box to expand.

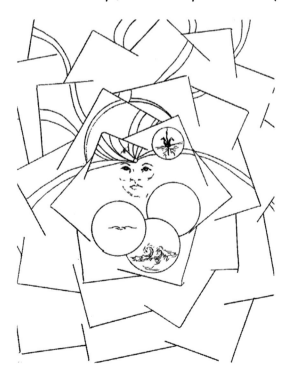

MESSAGE 83
CHANGE AND REALITY

Your scientists realize that the world that you know and the world that surrounds you are always in constant flux. There are multi-realities, multi-choices available every moment. Quantum Physics offers insights into these multidimensional realities. Quantum Physics shows that energy can be a particle or a wave.

Energy is imprinted by your conscious or unconscious thoughts. Each moment is new and fresh. It is awaiting your command. Humans are especially rigid with how they view their life, who they think they are, and how they should or shouldn't act or be.

Most humans are unaware that they imprint their reality each moment and they are locked into a mindset of beliefs that reality is always a certain way. Then it is so. They continue to create the same, again and again and again. It is an illusion that things stay the same. Your reality is always in flux.

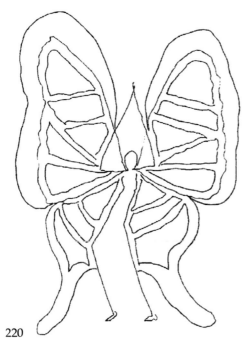

This imprinting of the energy field is done on an individual, collective basis. There are beliefs and certain types of rigid mindsets that exist in the collective consciousness of humanity. These beliefs and ways of being imprint the hologame, the matrix, the energy field, each moment. Therefore, the reality in which you play stays much the same.

There is comfort in the sameness. There is comfort in the belief of sameness. There is comfort in group beliefs, collective beliefs. It is a part of this planet's dysfunction.

Change is resisted because change is scary. Humans will hold on to a situation that is unhealthy and even painful because they are afraid of change. The collective consciousness acts much the same as the individuals.

Society sees and feels the dysfunctions. Society is challenged to make the conscious changes, especially when they are saturated with reasons to fear these changes. Each individual contributes their own personal fears, and insecurities to the whole. These collective fears, insecurities, and beliefs continue to keep the reality of dysfunction locked into each new now.

There is a gathering of those who are aware of the gift of imprinting each NOW with new realities. They are awakening to the realization that they are more than who they thought themselves to be. They are truly multidimensional beings, aware that reality is a thought, reality is a particle, and reality is a wave.

These beings are beginning to ride the energy in a new way. They are beginning to mold and sculpt their energy in a new way and therefore imprinting their reality with more loving consciousness.

It is an illusion that
things stay the same.
Your reality is always in flux.

Message 84
Self Healing Global Service

Everyone is being encouraged to transform their personal fear, personal righteousness, personal prejudice, personal rage and personal judgment.

Each individual, each human is responsible for the energy that they offer to the collective. Each individual, each human is being required to take their magnificent place in the transformation and unfolding of a better world—a world that knows peace, love and joy.

You must first have the conscious awareness of any behavior before you can transform that pattern or program. Until that awareness flashes into your conscious mind you are operating on automatic, your ego is in control and is driving your life.

The "out picturing" of the violence happening around the world is the collective emotional shadow of humanity. Humanity is awakening from a deep slumber, the ego slumber, the pre-patterned and pre-programmed slumber.

There is tremendous celestial support being offered to the personal and collective consciousness. This celestial support is assisting in the shift to the higher dimensions of freedom and flow—the dimensions in which all are aware "WE ARE ONE".

Each human carries an important key in this shift and transformation. Each human has an aspect of the collective shadow and can offer that shadow aspect to the light and transform what is repressed with an aware consciousness through their sacred heart.

It is your willingness, awareness, and asking for assistance in personal shadow work. It is dedication and diligence in healing, forgiving, and transforming all that has been repressed within the subconscious.

This is the opportunity of each multidimensional Star-being —
to transform their emotions, transform their frequencies and
transform their consciousness.

Each human is either imprinting this field of all possibility
with their fear, limiting beliefs and ego manipulation, or they
are imprinting this energy field with their love, joy, gratitude
and appreciation. Each human is a celestial transformer of
emotional energy.

Each human has an aspect of
the collective shadow and can offer that
shadow aspect to the light for transformation.

MESSAGE 85
CALL IT FORWARD

*E*ach new day is truly a gift that so often is put aside as you pick up the remains of yesterday. Remember that when old programs and doubts pop up you are offered the opportunity to transform that piece of emotional/mental dysfunctional energy.

You are transformers, pure and simple. You have the tools and the master keys of energetic alchemy. Every human is equipped with the awesome power to transform their reality. The shift and the transmutation of energy from patterns of dysfunction to patterns of empowerment and grace are an hourly, daily, and lifetime process.

There are those who embrace this shift and welcome it with open arms and there are those who resist every step of the evolutional path. They are engaged in the process of the struggle and it is the challenge of the struggle that makes them feel powerful and in control.

This is a false illusion. The power is in the trust and in the awareness of each moment, and in being in a gentle, alert, conscious state of mind. It is much like riding the wave, catching the wind in your sail, running the rapids.

If you could observe your cheering section of non-physical energy as you go about your interactions each day, you would be awesomely inspired.

Each human is the cutting edge of aware consciousness in physical form. The powers that each human has at their mental and emotional fingertips are truly incredible. You are the weavers, the creators, and the manfestants.

You are the extension of divine source in human form. Your life is the reflection of your skills and abilities.

224

The idea that you have a physical body and maintain that body is the first and most important aspect of manifesting.

Each human comes equipped with incredible capabilities. However, they use only a few of their awesome abilities. Each human has programs that veil and disguise their multidimensional talents. It is time to remove the veil and the dysfunctional disguises.

The concerns and worries hanging out in the edges of your consciousness are the remnants of the old patterns of helplessness, hopelessness and powerlessness. When they surface you have the opportunity to shift this dysfunctional pattern and choose another behavior, emotion, or thought to replace it.

This is a game, a hologame. Play it with joy and abandon. Play it with wonder and skill. Envision the most delicious possibilities reflected in your life. Imagine the very best result and call it forward. Your joy, gratitude and appreciation are the magnets which pull it to you.

You are the weavers, the creators, and the manifestants.

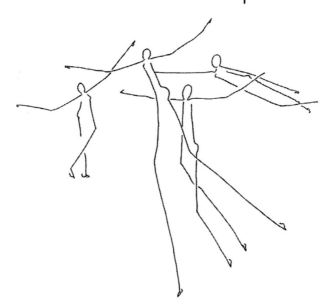

MESSAGE 86
MANIFESTANT

What is it to manifest? It is to reveal, to bring into light, to embody and materialize. We are aware that this sounds simple, and it is simple — when you are aware and know fully that you are pure spirit, pure consciousness, and pure energy.

Become aware that your pure spirit, pure consciousness and pure energy has been manipulated and programmed since the birth. This is the time for humanity to step out of the haze and numbness of powerlessness and fear, to shake off misconceptions and beliefs about lack and scarcity.

Each human carries some aspect of this limiting programming. These beliefs have been handed down from one generation to the next, sometimes in words, but more often in the energetic stance or energetic signatures of parents, teachers, leaders, employers, and the collective consciousness of the entire matrix.

The work for each human in this moment in time is to shake off this programming, lift consciousness and awareness up to the place of totally knowing who they are as a multidimensional starhuman.

Each human is unlimited, infinite, and powerful beyond measure. Each human is a creator, an energy vortex and a manifestant of the highest degree. Step into this knowing. Step into this awareness. Step into and embody this true clear power.

You and all others are transforming the remains of any dysfunctional patterns, beliefs and behaviors that are in your human operating system.

Scan your life, review and discover all the times when you asked and did receive. Make a list for yourself of the multitude of times you had a need or desire, asked for it and it appeared, it was revealed and made visible. You will discover through this process all the times in which you manifested your desires.

The last aspect of the cycle is to allow yourself to receive what you have asked for. Practice more allowing and practice more gratitude. Relax into the process and know that all is well and that all is unfolding as it should be.

Your beloved planet is embraced by the incredible infusion of the Divine Light of Awareness. When any bright light shines in a place that has been dark, all is revealed, and the dysfunctions and patterns that have been hidden in the shadows can be transformed as they are brought to awareness and full consciousness.

Each human is unlimited, infinite, and powerful beyond measure.

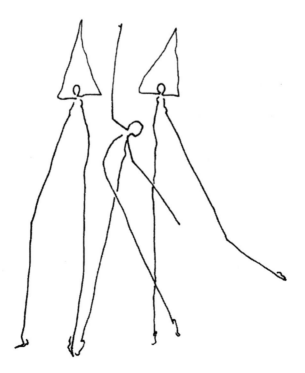

Message 87
Be in Joy

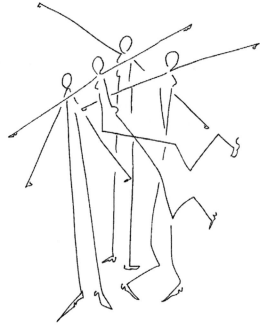

Joy is the elixir for all things. Bring more joy into your tasks. When you radiate a vibration of joy, however mild, there is a shift in response within your body that is reflected in the response of your reality.

It can be as easy as a smile on your face as you do one of your many tasks. This will create a different message to your body and you will shift the usual stress responses to your work and busyness into a more conscious relaxed state of mind/heart.

Become aware of the stages or subtle frequencies of the emotional vibration you label joy. There is ecstasy, rapture, bliss, jubilation, delight, happiness, cheer, gladness, and pleasure. Practice the different frequencies of joy.

Be delighted. Celebrate the small wonders all around you. Rejoice with your breath. Smile for no reason, just smile into the moment.

Allow new face muscles to be discovered as you smile into your concerns and worries.

Find cause to laugh, giggle, or radiate cheerfulness, practice being light-hearted, carefree, and elated about the miracles in your life or the miracles of the moment. Be happy, be bright, rejoice and enjoy. Be in Joy.

The skill of maintaining an attitude and frequency of joy is a most important skill. Imagine that you have a joy muscle and you have not exercised it enough. You need to stretch it, expand it and fully express it. Allow joy in any form to proceed you.

Smile as you answer the phone, make a meal, and pay your bills. Smile into the mirror each time you look at your image, smile at your reflection. Smile as you are falling asleep at night. Practice smiling even while you are thinking.

Place your awareness in your heart when you smile. This is a powerful alchemical practice. The simple act of smiling from your heart will attract more joy, bliss, and happiness into your life.

The physical tasks will flow easier, your body will respond by being relaxed with less stress. The worries will evaporate; the tasks will be completed with ease and grace. Joy will clear the way for incredible miracles and expansion. This is a wonderful skill to practice and use that will enhance everything in your life.

The energy field that radiates from joy will transform any experience, activity, outcome or results. Your joy will be like a healing balm to yourself and others in your life. Practice your joy in all is wondrous forms.

Practice being light-hearted.

MESSAGE 88
CLAIM YOUR GIFTS

We are here, streaming energy, offering suggestions and gentle reminders that you are a multidimensional being of great skill with a great desire to serve. These are miraculous, wondrous times. Humans are expanding into their full powerful potential as the multidimensional beings they truly are.

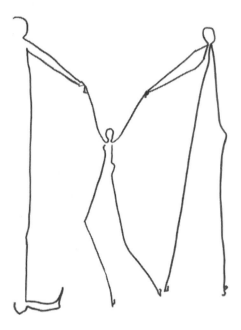

Your news offers examples of the incredible abilities of multidimensional beings, the story of the young blind man who senses sound vibrations bouncing off objects as he clicks like the dolphins. He has stepped into his potential functioning like a sighted person.

The psychologist who shared his story about the miraculous closing of the entire ward of declared criminally insane patients who were restored to balance. He was aware that by healing himself, it would offer the patients healing because he knew with certainty they were a part of him.

There is powerful potential within, which humans are discovering. Your reality is unlimited, infinite, ever expanding. Each day there is news which declares another wondrous, amazing ability that has been discovered and revealed by humans who are claiming their true identity and their multidimensional reality.

We wish you could only see yourselves as we do—bright oscillating frequencies of color and light, pure potential, pure creative energy. These are exciting times on your planet, an awakening, a turning, an expanding.

You have a front row seat. You have the winning ticket. You have the awesome opportunity to allow yourself to expand into your unlimited reality and unlimited ability to claim and own your multidimensional gifts.

• You are invited to release the old programs that limit your thinking.

• You are invited to release the old emotions that keep you vibrating in a dense form.

• You are invited to release the concepts of what you think is real.

• You are invited to step out of your self created, self imposed limitation box.

• You are invited to honor your magnificence every moment with every breath.

• You are invited to hold and radiate a pure frequency of joy, gratitude and appreciation.

• You are invited to stay in the chalice of your heart, offering compassion and forgiveness.

• You are invited to practice the frequency of pure love.

These suggestions will assist you in claiming the wonders of who you truly are as an emissary of the galaxy, as an aspect of the divine creator, as an aspect of the one cosmic heart.

Step into this day with a true sense of gratitude. Claim the magic and wonder that is yours. Breath life into your dreams, your moments, and make them gifts to one and all.

Be at peace, beloved.

We offer our gratitude to
those who hear or feel this call.

Our Invitation Continues...

We are here. We are available, simply by request. We stream to all those who invite our presence. We meet; we connect in the coherent energy field of the purest, highest frequency and vibration of joy, gratitude and appreciation.

We offer our gratitude to those who hear or feel this call. May our messages touch the hearts and minds of those willing to know who they truly are, magnificent multidimensional starhumans. It is through loving and awake hearts that transformation is made possible.

Each individual offers love, compassion, and acceptance, in a unique and fresh way. Some express their expanded multidimensional selfhood through their service work, their spoken or written words, their art or touch, all empowered with their heart focus and dedication.

Each offering infused with the pure, coherent emotions of joy, gratitude and appreciation has value and adds to the global collective. We are all one!

About the Author...

Peggy Black, Transducer, Scribe and Witness, is a world traveler and lecturer with thirty-five years experience in the healing field. She has been featured internationally in television, radio and print media. Peggy is a Multidimensional Channel whose gifts as a clairsentient, clairvoyant and clairaudient intuitive allow her to assist individuals to live empowered and abundant lives. Peggy receives transmissions from her "celestial team" which she calls the Morning Messages, inviting us to honor our multidimensional Self.

Sacred Sound Salutarist, Peggy uses powerful core sounds for vibrational healing. She is passionate about sharing the power of sound as a healing modality. She founded Sound Pod, and continues to create global community Sound Pods that empower others to freely use sound. She believes consciously intended sounds relieve stress, clear blockages and elevate awareness, promoting wholeness and healing.

Spiritual Synergist, she conducts ceremonies of transformation worldwide. Arabia, England, Ireland, Egypt, Japan and St. Lucia are a few of the sacred sites where ceremonies have been performed using the power of sound and the holiness of water. Peggy is the Seneschal for the Labyrinth in the Garden of the Beloved.

Peggy has presented at numerous events and conferences including Women of Vision and Action, Healing Our World, Kauai Wellness Expo, New England Sound Healing, World Sound Healing, and Global Sound. Peggy founded the International Sound Symposium. She offered sacred sounds for the Shamanic Journey tour in temples and the Great Pyramid in Egypt. She conducted morning forums at Tom Kenyon's Sound Healer's Trainings. She was Ceremonialist for the sacred water ceremony, Ocean of Gratitude Cruise with Dr. Masaru Emoto. She was featured in People magazine as "Fabulous over Sixty."

Peggy offers lectures and workshops: Miracles, Intentions and Manifestations, Allowing Prosperity, Sound Awareness, Sculpting Reality with Sound, The Power of Your Words and Intentions, The Creative You, and Engaging Celestial Support.

Peggy still lives in the home she built in the redwoods near Santa Cruz, CA. Contact her at www.peggyblack.com.

Acknowledgment and Support...

Motivational Press:
  Justin Sachs, www.Motivationalpress.com

Graphic Art and Design, Author:
  Melanie Gendron, www.melaniegendron.com

Rough Giraffe Productions CD and DVD Editing:
  Brian Todd, info@roughgiraffe.com

C&C Offset Printing Company:
  Vicki Lundgren, www.ccoffset.com

Webcast Host and Author:
  Randy Monk, www.TimelyGuidance.com

Webcast Hostess:
  Cyndi Silva, www.metaphysicalwisdom.com

Higher Speech:
  Datta Groover, www.Higherspeech.com

Intention Partners:
  New Perspectives, Ellen Henson, Ellen@lifeInsights.net
  Susanne Craig

Office Goddess:
  Nicole Morelli

Editing Support for the Eighty-eight Transmissions:
  LeAnn Meyers

Editing Support for the Invitations Deck:
  Jennifer Grady

Editing Support for Morning Message Books:
  Tom Johnson and Michael Ruggles

Founder of Healing Music:
  Amrita Cottrell, www.healingmusic.org

Founder of Shamanic Journeys and Author:
  Nicki Scully, www.shamanicjourneys.com

Founder of Healing Sounds and Authors:
  Jonathan and Andi Goldman, www.healingsounds.com

Founder of Author One Stop and Author:
   Randy Peyser, www.AuthorOneStop.com

Founder of Share Foundation and S.E.E Publishing, Author:
   Virginia Essene, www.virginiaessene.com

Founder of New Human Project and Author:
   Donna Aazura, www.donnaaazura.com

Glimpse into Another Reality and Author:
   Barbara Thomas, www.barbarathomas.info

Reality Shifter and Author:
   Cynthia Sue Larson, www.realityshifters.com

Cosmic Telepath and Author:
   Ronna Herman, www.AskArchangelMichael.com

Soul Purpose Living and Author:
   Kay Snow-Davis, www.SoulPurposeAcademy.com

Sacred Relationship and Authors:
   Jerry and Richela Chapman, www.sacredrelationship.com

Steward of Go Gratitude and Author:
   Stacey Robyn, www.gogratitude.com

Ocean of Gratitude:
   Karol Avalon, www.oceanofgratitudecruise.com

International Speaker and Author:
   Jill Lubin, www.jilllublin.com

Heartlites Incorporated, President/CEO:
   Marcy Neumann www.heartlitesinc.com

Marketing and Author:
   Peter Melton

Design Graphics:
   Michael Boyce

Flash Movie, LightWerxMedia:
   Trevor Thomas, www.lightwerxmedia.com

Website Design and Marketing, Author:
   Robert Evans, formerly Pass Along Concepts,
   now, The Messenger Network

More Offerings from Morning Messages...

Morning Messages "We Are Here" Transmissions Book includes the unfolding, miraculous story of the process and eighty-eight illustrated messages. These messages open new doors and bust down some of your old doors and beliefs. Each message will intrigue and invite you to practice fresh ways of looking at your life.

Morning Messages Invitations Book — forty-four invitations that will entice and summon you to step into a new way of responding to your life. Once you begin using these invitations, there will be no turning back. Your life will change. Your life will transform. You will begin to expect miracles every day.

"We Are Here" Transmissions, the Morning Messages — Double CD Set — The Audio version of the Morning Messages will give you a quick, vibrational frequency boost. Listen in the car, on the plane, as a meditation, when you need to remember your magnificence, or to maintain your high frequency of joy, gratitude and appreciation.

The Morning Messages Invitation Deck — 44 invitations offering consciousness exercises to support your well-being and expansion.

Celebrating the Morning Messages — DVD, 50 minute presentation: The Story, Heart Space, Celestial Partnership

Wisdom and Guidelines for Multidimensional Humans Poster
These eleven guidelines inspire and uplift. They offer a focus to shift our consciousness. They encourage us to remember that our thoughts, words, deeds and actions affect the whole.

Other 8.5x11 Inspirational Posters Available on Web Site

Join the Morning Message family — subscribe for the free 88 messages: www.morningmessages.com.

Peggy is available for personal channeled transmissions, lectures and workshops. These channeled readings offer insights and guidance to bring clarity to your personal challenges and questions — joyandgratitude@aol.com.

For information or inquiries about wholesale purchases, contact Peggy Black, 831-335-3145, or peggyblack@aol.com.

LaVergne, TN USA
20 September 2010

197632LV00008B/4/P